FROM DU BOIS TO OBAMA

FROM
DU BOIS
TO OBAMA

AFRICAN AMERICAN
INTELLECTUALS
IN THE
PUBLIC FORUM

CHARLES PETE BANNER-HALEY

Southern Illinois University Press
Carbondale and Edwardsville

13 12 11 10   4 3 2 1

Library of Congress Cataloging-in-Publication Data
Banner-Haley, Charles Pete T., 1948–
From Du Bois to Obama : African American intellectuals
in the public forum / Charles Pete Banner-Haley.
    p. cm.
Includes bibliographical references and index.
ISBN-13: 978-0-8093-2979-3 (cloth : alk. paper)
ISBN-10: 0-8093-2979-4 (cloth : alk. paper)
ISBN-13: 978-0-8093-8562-1 (ebook)
ISBN-10: 0-8093-8562-7 (ebook)
1. African Americans—Intellectual life—20th century.
2. African Americans—Intellectual life—21st century.
3. African American intellectuals. 4. African American
leadership. 5. African Americans—Civil rights—History. 6. African Americans—Race identity. 7. United
States—Intellectual life. 8. United States—Race relations. I. Title.
E185.89.I56B36 2010
323.1196'073—dc22   2009037550

In dedication and thanks to
Ralph Watkins, 1943–2007

CONTENTS

PREFACE

When I first set out to write about African American intellectuals, I was considering a straightforward narrative of who was who in the long struggle to point out and/or frame the discussion of the conditions and experience of black Americans. That notion very quickly went by the wayside as I realized that in the late twentieth century, African American intellectuals were not only a visible entity but also influential in the general intellectual discourse of the nation. The reasons for this were many, but in the end, the consideration of them led me to the writing of this book. In short, those reasons had to do with the success of integration owing to the Civil Rights movement on creating a large and solid black professional middle class, a general shift in the demographics of the nation that has challenged the racial formation of what the American identity is about, and the perennial but now seemingly decisive role that African American cultural productions have played in the last half century of America's history.

To that end I have framed this book as a series of historical meditations on what it has meant to be an African American intellectual from the era of the Great Depression to the historic moment of the election and inauguration of the United States' first black American president. Of course that election was the furthest thing from my mind as I read the various intellectuals covered in this book. But, given the dramatic changes that have occurred over the last seventy-odd years, the election of Barack Obama owes much to the piercing insights and steady growth in visibility and influence of African American public intellectuals. It is certainly no accident that Obama himself is an intellectual who has learned much from those who came before him. As I learned, the major black intellectual who overshadows all black public intellectuals in the twentieth and twenty-first centuries is W. E. B. Du Bois. His genius and expansive mind laid the groundwork that all black intellectuals across the spectrum of ideology or disciplinary leanings must work through. Needless to say, I remain in awe of his immense intellectual prowess and influence.

This book has many people for whom I am in great debt. Of course the assessments here are my own and they bear no burden of responsibility for my renderings. To that end I wish to thank, for their encouragement and stimulating conversations about black intellectuals and the life of the nation in general, Robin D. G. Kelley, William Julius Wilson, David Levering Lewis, Trudier Harris-Lopez, Darlene Clark Hine, Stephanie Shaw, Patricia Williams, Eugene D. Genovese and the late Elizabeth Fox-Genovese, Mark M. Smith, David Chappell, Louis Ferleger, Jay Mandle, Joan Mandle, Rhonda Levine, Julius Lester, Arnold Rampersad, Adolph L. Reed, Reverend Eugene Rivers III, Randall Kennedy, Larry Greene, Barbara Jeanne Fields, Julie Saville, and Daryl Michael Scott. There have been many others too numerous to name here, but they should know that my gratitude and indebtedness goes out to them.

The staffs at the Spingarn-Moorland Research Center at Howard University and the Schomburg Center for Black Culture in New York City have been immensely helpful in getting rare books and papers of some of the events and intellectuals that I discuss. This research was aided by generous grants for my home institution, Colgate University. It was also at Colgate that I was able, with the inspiration and help of Roy Bryce La-Porte, to inaugurate a series of lectures by leading African American intellectuals in honor of W. E. B. and Shirley Graham Du Bois during the 1990s.

My students, over the years that this book was being written, were very helpful in their thoughts, comments, and in some cases research into certain parts of this book. In particular I would like to thank Vicky Chung for her gathering of information on Asians and African Americans in California during the 1930s. Many thanks for the following students for their comments in classes I have taught on black intellectuals and the Civil Rights movement and during office hours: Breanna Johnson, Christopher Ekpo, Kia King, Erin Lyons, Gabrielle Casey-Jones, Lynne Ai, "JJ" Hackett, Alexandra Wolters, Paige Carlos, Daniel Cantor, and Jacqueline Adlam. Again there have been so many others who could be mentioned but they, too, have my thanks.

As this book went to Southern Illinois University Press, I must thank Sylvia Frank Rodrigue for her unflagging encouragement and friendship in the arduous process of bringing this book to the light of publication. Likewise, the anonymous readers are to be thanked for their comments and suggestions that have made this work stronger. In addition, I would like to thank Brigette Wiksten and Karl Kageff for their help with the notes and bibliography. I must also thank Denise, who has shared my life for many years and has lived through the ups and downs of the research and writing of this book. As ever, she has been angelic.

This book of course is not the final word on African American intellectuals. If anything it is but a modest effort to move and perhaps widen the conversation. In the long run it will hopefully inspire more works in an already growing field.

This book is dedicated to my teacher, mentor, and friend in African American history, Ralph Watkins (1943–2007). Ralph, like those above, and I had many conversations over the years about African American intellectuals, and he knew of my intense interest in another area that I was working, a history of African Americans in upstate New York. In both areas, he was of immeasurable help and guidance. He is and will be sorely missed.

INTRODUCTION: WHAT IS AN AFRICAN AMERICAN INTELLECTUAL?

The question of what is an African American intellectual seems so simple that it obscures the complexity of its answer. Most people would quickly answer that an African American intellectual is a black American who has pondered the black experience in America and has proffered some analysis, commentary, and perhaps some particular solutions for the improvement and advancement of the race.

If it were that simple, then there would not be a burgeoning subfield in African American history given to the study of African American intellectual history. There certainly would not be important books that have surveyed black intellectuals over time, critiqued the political engagement of African American intellectuals, brooded over the crisis of black intellectuals, and analyzed the "dilemma" of the black intellectual. However path breaking, flawed, or persuasive these works are, they do more to show the complexity of African American intellectuals rather than state precisely what an African American intellectual is.[1]

If we go beyond the simple definition recited above, we can expand the meaning by looking at space, place, and change. In other words, an African American intellectual occupies a particular space in a particular place or places and, like most people and circumstances, changes over time. This expanded definition is more grounded historically than, say, a definition that is grounded in political typology, philosophical categories, or even an economic paradigm.[2]

An African American intellectual dealing with issues affecting black America in the 1930s occupied a particular space within an America that was a segregated society by law and after the fact. That intellectual would be out of space and place in the 1980s, the 1990s, and into the twenty-first century. Indeed, African American intellectuals of the 1930s would share, perhaps, an ongoing conversation over the roles that class and race play affecting the conditions of black people. But the changes over time have reshaped that conversation such that E. Franklin Frazier's bitter indictment of the black bourgeoisie has been replaced by works that examine and analyze the emergence, in the last forty-five years, of the largest black middle class in African American history. Where sociologist Oliver C. Cox presented a Marxian analysis of racism and white power in the 1930s and 1940s, by the beginning of the twenty-first century, Thomas C. Holt was offering a critical examination of race, power, and class that was conscious of the collapse of state communism in Russia, its softening in China, and its isolation in Cuba.[3]

And yet there are constant issues that African American intellectuals have had to grapple with over time. The most tenacious, and many would say most pernicious, is race. Historically in the United States race has been bound up with slavery. African-descended people have been cast as "other" even as their bodies and souls were used to build a powerful nation that held a deep belief in the ideas of democracy, equality, and freedom. It has taken three revolutions to painfully reach some tangible reality of these ideas, and still, race, culture, and ethnicity menace the land negatively, create rifts that resist reconciliation, and close off that much needed dialogue that African American intellectuals seek to make some sort of resolution. Thomas C. Holt presented the matter aptly: "Both race and culture, then, share ambiguous boundaries and both race and ethnicity are socially constructed identities. Once we recognize this we immediately confront the fact that both must be historically contingent, and if they are historical, then their further analysis requires mapping the relations of power, the patterns of construction, and struggle out of which such social constructions emerge."[4]

This, of course, is what African American intellectuals have attempted to do. In some ways it also defines who they are. If we understand that an intellectual is more than someone who loves "the life of the mind" and is ensconced at far remove from the public, then we come closer to knowing what an Afro-American intellectual is. Better still is Michel Foucault's general definition of the public intellectual: "The role of the intellectual is not to tell others what they have to do. [It is] to question over and over again what is postulated as self-evident, to disturb people's mental habits, the way they do and think certain things, to dissipate what is familiar and accepted, to reexamine rules and institutions."[5]

Foucault's definition can be modified (and clarified) to address African American intellectuals. First, black intellectuals have, from the past into the present, told the black masses and the rest of America what they must do. There is an earnest moral undertone to African American intellectuals' prescriptions, whether it is religious or secular or political or all three. Secondly, given the struggles to understand, fight, and eradicate racism, African American intellectuals have occupied a unique position within the society to not only "disturb people's mental habits" and the way things are done and accepted but to envision how American could be a truly democratic, diverse, equal, and free land.

Intellectuals in modern times (that is, those historical periods of industrialization and urbanization) whether positively or negatively represent a force in society that generates debate, policy, and change. Optimistically, that change leads to a progression toward the best that society can be. African American intellectuals operate in a similar fashion but with these specific additions: they act as a moral force to get America to embrace its past, to become more inclusive and accepting of humanity, to take responsibility for social justice. Whether the goal was ending segregation and lynching in pursuit of equal opportunities in the 1930s, to the freedom marches in the 1950s and 1960s, to 1980s and 1990s struggles with the perennial facts of police brutality, drugs, and violent sectors of the society trafficking in racial hatred, African American intellectuals have drawn on the past to remind the populace of what has occurred and what can be done. They have called upon the great principles of this nation to cajole the United States to better itself through inclusion and diversity. And perhaps most importantly, African American intellectuals have been and are seekers of truth about humanity and social justice.

All intellectuals who are engaged in that universal quest for the meaning of life and its essential truths sometimes stumble down wrong paths and fall under the sway of seductive but ultimately wrongheaded ideas. These ideas can often be corrected through honest reflection and self-criticism. W. E. B. Du Bois was a sterling example of an intellectual who constantly wrestled with what it meant to be black and American. It was one of the central motifs of his intellectual life. Wilson Jeremiah Moses, a prominent scholar of African American intellectual history observed that Du Bois's intellectual grappling with what today we would call Afrocentrism "exposed numerous conflicts within his own complex identity. There was warfare between his loyalties as a social democrat and racial romantic, another battle between his im-

3

pulses as traditionalist and iconoclast. There was a tension between his austerity and his enthusiasm, another between his elitism and his folkishness, and yet another between his blatant Prussianism and his latent bohemianism."[6]

Such tensions led Du Bois to advocate by turns a pan-Africanism that veered closer to Marcus Garvey's separatist ideal than he might have admitted. Though he believed in integration, Du Bois also believed in the necessity and worth of black institutions and the black church. In the 1930s, as he wrote a serious Marxian influenced revisionist history of Reconstruction, Du Bois embroiled himself in a deep controversy over his call for African Americans to form a separate economy.[7]

Du Bois looms large as to what an African American intellectual is. His presence, strong and enduring as it is, however, must not be allowed to overshadow all those other black American men and women whose ideas, critical analyses, and intellectual creativity have moved American civilization to higher levels of respectability, cultural achievements, and social responsibility. Zora Neale Hurston, Richard Wright, and Ralph Ellison were African American writers whose work was steeped in intellectual inquiry into the meaning of the black experience in America. For Hurston, who studied anthropology under Franz Boas while attending Barnard College, Negro folklore was seen as a central feature of Southern black rural life that was rapidly disappearing. Though a member of the Harlem Renaissance, Hurston was iconoclastic and sought to heighten the individualistic ethos in that movement as opposed to the celebratory or, later, protest writing concerning the collective accomplishments or cruel victimization of the race.[8]

Richard Wright, brought up in harsh poverty of segregated Mississippi, struggled mightily to overcome those conditions and upon reaching the North grew into a man of serious thought. His short stories *Uncle Tom's Children* and first novel, the Book-of-the-Month Club selection *Native Son,* were solid intellectual achievements as well as literary successes. Looking at rural Southern black folk life through an existentialist and social realist lens, *Uncle Tom's Children* laid bare the thinking of a man whose brushes with racism in the South scarred him deeply. In *Native Son*, Wright brought a different focus to black urbanization. Here, in the ghetto, in the character of Bigger Thomas, we are presented with a black nationalism that is at once existentialist and violent. White America created Bigger, and in his anger, he lashes out for freedom through murder not only of whites but of blacks.[9]

Richard Wright's characters can be seen as studies in victimization, at least from the vantage point of the present, with its preoccupation with identity politics and overheated discussions about victimization of black people by white racism. But within the context of its time, Wright's novel *Native Son* departed from the politically charged proletarian writings of the 1930s to present a more nuanced reading of Depression-era pre–World War II black urban America. On the one hand, Wright presented a stereotypical story of the very thing that black intellectuals then, and now, fight against: the black man as a murderous beast. On the other hand, Wright wrote an eerily prescient book (based, incidentally, on an actual occurrence) that shows what happens when America excludes and demeans blacks and then attempts through liberal guilt and radical engineering to rehabilitate them. Either way the novel is approached, there is an intellectual challenge that goes to the core of what constitutes an African American intellectual.

Ralph Ellison, Wright's one-time protégé and good friend, followed with an artistic endeavor that presented another intellectual challenge. *Invisible Man* (1952) was published in the midst of the Cold War and on the cusp of the dramatic revolution that would present African America with its greatest opportunity for freedom and equality since Reconstruction. Ralph Ellison's panoramic, jazz-inflected story of one man's search for identity and meaning in an America that transforms and reinvents itself was not only an attempt at literary greatness. It was also an intellectual meditation on the meaning of American history and culture and the centrality of African Americans to both.

Ellison's background provided him with a unique vantage point from which to map out his ideas. While a Southerner like his contemporaries Richard Wright and Zora Neale Hurston, Ellison grew up in Oklahoma (the "Territory") where there was a confluence of Native American, African American, and European American people before statehood brought Jim Crow segregation and increasing racial violence.[10] Always well-read, Ellison's initial desire was to be a musician and a composer. Torn between wanting to play jazz and becoming a classical composer, Ellison's aesthetic and intellectual struggle mirrored that of many black intellectuals who found themselves conflicted by a desire to embrace black folk culture (whether rural or urban), a desire that was criticized if not outright condemned by black educators, ministers, and parents who wanted their young people to cultivate higher, more respectable forms of culture. It is no exaggeration to say that 1930s jazz and 1940s and '50s bebop are akin to 1980s and '90s rap and hip-hop in the reception they received from black middle-class professionals and parents.

For Ralph Ellison, jazz was an American music that was emblematic of a miscegenated society. Blacks and whites could play jazz because it came out of the soil that had been worked by black slaves, that had been bloodied by a war between the states that cost white and black lives in a struggle to end slavery and elevate freedom for black people. Yet for all of that, white Americans continued to render African Americans invisible.

It was not so much a veil that was erected, as so many black intellectuals, notably Du Bois, had stated. For Ellison, it was more a conscious denial of black people's presence in the nation and its history. Near the end of the twentieth century, another black writer and intellectual, Julius Lester, echoed this notion of denial. "At the center of our nation's history," Lester observed, "lies the black presence, a presence with which the non-black majority has never found the means to be comfortable." Lester stated that one of the important aspects of twentieth-century American history was "the effort made by whites to come to terms with that black presence."[11]

What an African American intellectual is, then, is a person who reveals what America truly is. Whether the tools are the novelist's assembling words to expose those truths or the sociologist's piercing examination to illuminate color and caste within and without African America or the historian's relentless pursuit to recover the *whole* story of America by placing blacks in the central narrative, the goal is to demolish denial; to replace invisibility with visibility and to move the nation through the realization of social justice and responsibility to the fulfillment of the American creed.

If the Revolutionary War set the foundations of the American creed with its idea of a Constitution granting liberty, justice, and the pursuit of happiness and the Civil War and Reconstruction attempted to root out the flaws—slavery and inequality based on race—then the Civil Rights revolution moved the United States yet further toward the realization of freedom, equality, and the pursuit of happiness (read here as the creation of the good society). Whether it was the words and actions of Martin Luther King Jr. and the SCLC (Southern Christian Leadership Conference) or the courageous activities of the young people, black and white, in SNCC and CORE (Student Nonviolent Coordinating Committee and Congress of Racial Equality), the ideas of a beloved community overcoming racial injustice and creating a participatory democracy inspired people to seek to redefine power arrangements in American society. The movement attempted to fundamentally change the ways in which America views its people, its manners of equity, and its inattention to those whose voices had long gone unheard.

As momentous as that revolution was, however, the Civil Rights movement at once settled scores that the failure of Reconstruction incurred and set into motion waves of changes that amounted to a redefining of America so as to be more inclusive, integrative, and equitable politically, socially, and economically. All of these changes have, of course, not yet occurred. Indeed, there still exists much contention over whether affirmative action represents reparations for centuries of discrimination against African Americans and what that means ultimately for the political economy. In like manner, if the Civil Rights movement sought a harmonious community based upon openness and inclusion, African American intellectuals now had to confront new definitions of identity and race. This last was the result of the emergence of the largest black professional middle class in the nation's history and was further compounded by the steady influx of immigrants from the Caribbean, Africa, and Asia. Even more historically momentous was the election of the first black American to the presidency in 2008. Barack Hussein Obama in many ways was a culmination of the Civil Rights movement and starting point for African American intellectuals to confront those new definitions of race and identity.

By the early beginnings of the twenty-first century, Hispanics were officially declared the largest minority in America. While this seemed to bode ill for black Americans politically as the major political parties moved to court the Latino vote, culturally African Americans permeated and changed the American landscape. Whether it be rap and hip-hop, recognition by the Academy Awards in motion pictures, or a high visibility on television (not only in series programming but also in commercials), African Americans for the first time were defining their place and presence in American culture.

But the redefining promises to grow even more complicated. A quick look at popular culture clearly shows that black intellectuals in the late twentieth and early twenty-first centuries took on the role of celebrated (if not celebrity) public intellectuals. Whether it was Michael Eric Dyson articulating a post-integration black postmodernism, or Robin D. G. Kelley exhorting young blacks to creatively and radically dream of black freedom while using the past as a guide and teacher, or Toni Morrison showing how "Africanness is inextricably intertwined with Americaness," or Henry Louis Gates Jr. bringing Du Bois's long-planned Africana encyclopedia into fruition, these black intellectuals brought African America into visibility. These intellectuals mirrored what Aaron McGruder's syndicated comic strip and later television show *The Boondocks* humorously though critically commented upon regarding race, identity, hip-hop, politics, and America in general.[12]

The main difference between McGruder's comic strip, often compared to Gary Trudeau's *Doonesbury*, and the other intellectuals is that McGruder, who identifies with the Left, is unafraid to criticize the black Left. Indeed all manner of black folks come under heavy scrutiny, from rappers to politicians to popular movie and television stars.[13] But McGruder's particular intellectual activism operates within a political culture and across an ideological spectrum that displays African American intellectuals more visibly than at any other time in American history. In the post-integration era of the late twentieth and early twenty-first centuries, it can no longer be said that African American intellectuals are generally male and left-oriented. The strong presence of African American women in intellectual quarters since at least the 1970s has decisively challenged the dominant masculinist aura in black intellectual discourse. African American women intellectuals such as Beverly Guy-Sheftall, bell hooks, Patricia Hill Collins, Hazel Carby, Alice Walker, Pauli Murray, Audre Lorde, June Jordan, Trudier Lopez-Harris, and Hortense Spillers, among others, have analyzed, critiqued, and moved black intellectual discourse a long ways toward recognizing not only women's voices and concerns but also the important intersections of race, gender, sex, class, and politics that face African Americans, indeed, all Americans in the new century.

In a simplistic way, African American intellectuals who call for a "color-blind society" that moves beyond playing the race card or playing the victim are often called conservative. Shelby Steele, John Mc-Whorter, and the dean of late twentieth-century black conservatism, Thomas Sowell, would certainly fit this simple definition. But matters of intellectual discourse are never simple. Sowell and Steele came up during the revolutionary fires of the 1960s Civil Rights and Black Power movements. Like many young African Americans of that period, they flirted with the cultural notions of black pride and the political ideas of black nationalism. In the end (more quickly for Sowell than Steele), they took up traditional conservative and neoconservative stances regarding their place in the United States. For both men, race was of little concern when it came to being an American. It certainly was irrelevant to seizing opportunities for achievement and character building. For black conservatives, including Sowell and Steele, the Civil Rights movement succeeded: all that needed to be done was to adhere to the principles they saw reiterated by Martin Luther King Jr. Black conservatives called for judgment by the content of one's character rather than the color of one's skin, the removal of all suggestions of race, race classification, and, finally elimination of affirmative action because of their stigmatizing effects on black individuals' advancement. These issues became the hallmarks of the new black conservatives.[14]

If King was appropriated to deliver the new black conservative message, then the door was open to bringing in Frederick Douglass and W. E. B. Du Bois into the fold. Douglass's fervent belief in racial amalgamation and the creation of an "American race" seemed to comport well with black and white conservatives eager to relinquish ideas and discussions about race. John McWhorter even moved to adopt Du Bois's double-consciousness theorem to show that blacks still have double consciousness, only in a post-integration mode. Inwardly, (middle-class) black people know that race is irrelevant and that they have succeeded but outwardly they hold whites accountable for continued racism and oppression. The new black bourgeoisie seemingly cannot let go of race and racism as a badge of identity and authenticity.[15]

From the vantage point of African American intellectual history, present-day black conservatives are blind to their past. There have always been black intellectuals who espoused a character-based, moral, and meritocratic ideology. The 1920s and '30s saw black individuals such as Kelly Miller, Charles S. Johnson, Nannie Burroughs, and George Schuyler to name but a few who believed in building the content of one's character, morally and productively, while battling racial discrimination. The key difference between those conservatives and conservatives now was that the former had to deal with a strict color line that was pervasive throughout the country (albeit more covert in the North). Jim Crow segregation in the South and the belief throughout the United States that most black people were incapable of doing, thinking, or even caring for themselves gave way to the "invisibility factor" regarding the African American presence in America. Thus behind the veil, a Kelly Miller or a Nannie Burroughs would most certainly call for political actions that would erase the color line even as they saw themselves as Americans entitled to all the opportunities that the American creed entailed. Remove the veil, grant the rights through legal means that would remove the color line, and what you would have, apparently, would be an African America more American and in line with the rest of the nation; race would not create divisiveness or violence, politically, economically, and socially. And the new black conservatives would now just be conservatives.

But even as the above is committed to print, historical knowledge of African Americans demolishes any effort to discard race from what it means to be an American, as well as what it means to be an African American intellectual. Many of the stances of black conservatism, in its ahistoricity, continue to contribute to white supremacy's moral ideology that blacks are incapable of thinking for themselves, have no history of any meaningful value, and are culturally degraded. Honest black conservatism does deal with race even as it seeks to relegate race to the margins of day-to-day living.

Where the African American leftist intelligentsia wants to confront racism through historical interrogation and analysis of structural impediments with an eye toward eventual eradication of racism morally and politically, the black intellectual Right would rather place the eradication of race and racism on the individual through the home, the church, and the school. And some black conservatives, seeing the successes that have come from the civil rights acts of over a generation ago, even believe that black suburbs with high-quality black schools that offer responsible values and a work ethic can work toward removing the need for affirmative action and the adoption of the roles of stigmatization and victimization.

Never before in African American history has the intellectual discourse been so rich with promise and so fraught with contention. The dramatic changes that have occurred since the 1930s, where this book begins, to the early years of the twenty-first century are a testament to the strength and contribution of a people who have integrally defined what it means to be African American and American.

This book is a meditative journey through the intellectual history of black American intellectuals. It seeks, as does all history, to help us understand where we are and why we are. How have we changed from the 1930s, when hope and despair seesawed for African American intellectuals, to the postwar 1950s, when black intellectuals were caught up in one of the first cultural shifts (some would say "wars") that would seek to define what American culture is? The 1960s represented another cultural and political shift as the veil was torn asunder and a new future for African American intellectuals opened into the final years of the twentieth century. The questions of race and color, identity politics, and the authenticity of black culture loomed large in these years as African American intellectuals and black Americans in general became more visible to all of America. Finally, perhaps the most historically significant occurrence, the election of Barack Obama to the American presidency, promises to open an even more challenging discourse for African American intellectuals.

[1] THE EMERGENCE OF THE BLACK PUBLIC INTELLECTUAL: RACE, CLASS, AND THE STRUGGLE AGAINST RACISM

The Great Depression caused deep stirrings in African America. By 1930, unemployment among black people in urban areas was on the increase. By 1932, joblessness would be greater than for the white populace, which also experienced steep increases. In some cities, Philadelphia to take but one example, more than half of the African American workforce had no work. Similar statistics could be seen across the nation. In more rural areas, particularly in the South, where poverty was common, the Depression only deepened it. Added to that was harsh Jim Crow segregation, which had been in force since the late nineteenth century. This segregation had drawn a porous but discernible veil throughout the South and other parts of the nation that rendered black Americans second-class citizens at best and invisible inferiors, vulnerable to violence against them, at worst.[1]

The "color line" and its attendant social mores and laws produced a culture in the South that attempted (and mostly succeeded) to place the lives of the region's people on a binary plane. Black was bad and white was good. As simple as it sounds, it was, of course, far more complicated. Just as the years of slavery saw evolutions in the behavior of the masters and the enslaved, Jim Crow segregation, by 1930 just over a generation old, was also evolving. What African Americans had to contend with in the South was a closed system that punished anyone who crossed the line or missed the cues of racial etiquette. Richard Wright of Mississippi certainly found this out. So did a young Ralph Ellison as he traveled by train from Oklahoma to Tuskegee, Alabama, to attend college.[2]

But the realities that Wright and Ellison faced are mere glimpses of what black Southerners faced day in and day out. The black world during segregation made do through its educational and religious institutions. In the cities, on the black side of town, a young child could see a world that held barbershops, pool halls, night clubs, funeral homes, houses of prostitution, insurance companies, as well as the aforementioned churches and schools. This black child may have seen a black physician when ill or visited relatives in the country during the summer. That child may have been of the small black middle class in their particular community or, more likely, had parents who were workers. Whatever the class, notwithstanding the important distinctions that class status held, the one thing that this child had in common with other black children was the fact of segregation and the barriers of racial discrimination that closed the opportunities and privileges to them that those on the other side of the color line, in white America, had.

Since the end of Reconstruction, black America found itself shut off from the victories attained after the Civil War and its Reconstruction aftermath. Despite the political successes that had occurred, the rapid rise in literacy, and that brief moment in the sunshine of equality and freedom, to paraphrase W. E. B. Du Bois's eloquent summation in his revisionist history *Black Reconstruction* (1935), by the 1930s a stranger to that history would never had suspected that dynamic movement among African Americans or their contributions to bringing a multiracial democracy into being. Even a New Negro renaissance in the 1920s, which showcased the best and brightest of black America's artists, writers, and intellectuals, was, to white America, more of an exotic show, an urban entertainment that offered a release through song and dance.

But for the New Negro's architects and participants, the movement was anything but exotic or playtime. This movement was a fresh chance to integrate the United States through popular culture and demonstrate the centrality of African Americans to the American enterprise. Black art, in the minds of African American intellectuals such as Du Bois and Alain Locke, would show America a worthy black African past even as black Americans moved toward what Ross Posnock has termed a "deracialized discourse." The preoccupation of the New Negro movement with race and culture and its meaning and effect on America as a whole became one pillar that black intellectuals would continue to grapple with for the rest of the twentieth century and into the twenty-first.[3]

The question of how to combat the poisonous effects of racist ideology and move beyond race was a defining one for black artists and intellectuals in the 1920s. On the one hand there was the need to see "Negroness" in a positive light, to recognize that there was a worthy historical past that was integral to U.S. history. The pioneer historian in this direction was Carter G. Woodson. Using the best methods of the progressive school of history, Woodson and his associates wrote empirical studies that examined African Americans regionally, nationally, and globally. Woodson was determined to place the contributions of black Americans before all of America and to instruct the black masses about their history in order to legitimate their claim to being bona fide American citizens.[4]

W. E. B. Du Bois certainly shared these notions, and his historical and sociological studies bear that out. It was Du Bois who laid down the main tenet of the African American dilemma: the double consciousness that permeated the black presence in America. It was a stunning concept when proposed in his 1903 classic *The Souls of Black Folks,* but it was, and is, a fluid and, therefore, slippery intellectual construction.[5] The double consciousness or "two-ness" idea had its roots in a racialist proposition that could be first seen in Du Bois's 1897 address to the American Negro Academy titled "The Conservation of the Races." A different version of this paper appeared in the *Atlantic Monthly* and a final version appeared in *Souls of Black Folks.* In the journey from an address to an academy of black intellectuals to a nationally published essay in a book, the heavy racialist tone was reduced to a somber meditation of what it means to be a black American. But between the lines, it could also be read as a serious reconsideration of what it meant to be an American.[6]

African American intellectuals then and now have debated the meanings and the value of Du Bois's double-consciousness theorem. Like many of Du Bois's works, it continues to fascinate, puzzle, and delight those who engage it. There can be no doubt that W. E. B. Du Bois was then and continues to be a towering intellect in African American and American life. As he worked through the 1920s pushing the idea that civil rights could be attained through a cultural renaissance, Du Bois was aware that there were other aspects of society that would have to change. Those parts included the economy, political attentiveness to black needs, and push to provide quality education and leadership to advance the race. There was also the need for fresh ideas and leaders to push for these changes. The Great Depression, which affected African America first and hardest, by the early 1930s brought those ideas and leaders to the forefront.[7]

The move of black intellectuals from invisibility to visibility was greatly aided by a shaken confidence in the ability of a capitalist political economy to maintain a stable and prosperous society. While capitalism, the driving economic engine of American society, had periodically experienced slumps and recoveries, the Great Depression demonstrated that serious flaws in the system existed. By 1933, four years after the crash, the Depression was ruining the banking system, farms were being devastated by overproduction, and the consumption of factory-produced goods (cars, radios, and so forth) by Americans had reached the point of diminishing return. On all levels and in almost every part of the economy, the United States plunged into what seemed to be an irreversible downslide. What made matters worse was that this depression was global. Every major world power was suffering from a financial downturn. That the Soviet Union, with its communist ideology and state control of production and agriculture, escaped the harshness of the downturn caused some European countries and some groups in America to consider socialism and communism as viable alternatives. Among black intellectuals, a young group of academically trained sociologists, political scientists, and economists embraced these alternatives and attempted to apply them toward solving not only the economic plight in America but also the racial dilemma.[8]

Intellectual historian Jonathan Scott Holloway examined in depth three of the better known "young Turks": economist Abram Harris, sociologist E. Franklin Frazier, and political scientist Ralph Bunche. The three were forbearers of what in the later part of the twentieth century would be known as black public intellectuals. As Holloway notes, "Teaching at Howard University from the late 1920s to the early 1940s, Harris, Frazier, and Bunche were pioneering social scientists and worked steadily to, if in different ways, reorient America's obsession with the Negro Problem away from an answer based upon racial solutions toward one grounded in class dynamics."[9]

The focus on class over race was certainly ahead of its time but not out of step with the alternatives that some more left-minded Americans were considering. What was significant about these three men's approach was the fact that they were African American; Frazier and Harris were Southerners while Bunche was a Midwesterner who moved to the West in his younger years; all disdained racial essentialism in general and that racial chauvinism associated with the New Negro movement in particular.

Their views were represented at the Second Amenia Conference in 1933 at Troutbeck, the estate of NAACP founder Arthur Spingarn.

The conference was called by W. E. B. Du Bois, who understood that African Americans had to embrace economic solutions in order to alleviate the effects of the Depression and to combat the pervasive racial inequality in the nation. Du Bois, working on a revisionist history of Reconstruction, had been immersing himself in Marxist ideas. While he was not quite ready to plunge into a thorough analysis that placed class above race, Du Bois recognized that American capitalism had devastated black America to the point of seemingly irreversible damage. In Du Bois's view—one that would ignite bombshells throughout the established organizations pursuing integration, especially the NAACP—perhaps it was time for African Americans to come together, build strong cooperative economic institutions, and create a competitive structure that would lead to equality. Mixed in this notion of economic cooperatives and self-segregation was a Marxian idea of building a class structure that would maintain an educated leadership class ("the talented tenth") and a hard-working, proud, and prosperous black working class that was not dependent on the vagaries of American corporate capitalism. Du Bois's distrust of any coalition between white and black workers led him down this path. Likewise, he hesitated in embracing the Communist Party's affirmation of such an alliance.[10]

The controversy over Du Bois's shift in thinking has bedeviled black intellectuals through the years. At the time, Du Bois called for "segregation and self-respect," principally to fight the deepening impoverishment of black people caused by the Depression. Integration, cultural or economic, did not make sense because African Americans had too few resources to achieve full equality. Setting aside the cultural pride that he fervently advocated in the second and third decades of the twentieth century, Du Bois was now more earnestly focused on the push to advance African Americans economically.[11]

Thus Du Bois was eager to hear and learn from the younger generation and their ideas about the situation. Where the First Amenia Conference addressed decidedly racial issues and called for racial solidarity among black leaders and a nod toward pan-Africanism (carried out mostly by Du Bois), the Second Amenia Conference focused on class. But clearly there were tensions at this meeting. Some were, as James O. Young has pointed out, generational differences between the class-conscious younger conferees and the race-minded leadership of the NAACP. Other tensions revolved around an exact rendering of class analysis. Abram Harris, E. Franklin Frazier, and Ralph Bunche took class analysis seriously; Harris had been a Communist Party member and all three eschewed race essentialism. They and others viewed Du Bois's interpretation of Marx as vulgar. Moreover, the young Turks were not afraid of alliances between black and white workers. Indeed, it was a cornerstone of their thinking. Labor and class had to transcend race. An international labor movement with class consciousness would ultimately solve the race problem and provide an alternative socioeconomic system.[12]

Perhaps the greatest irony of all could be found in the Left's, particularly the Communist Party's, favoring of a race essentialism based on an authentic oppositional black culture as formulated in the Comintern's 1928 "Black Belt thesis." The Third International had been sufficiently persuaded by a number of black intellectuals, including some who visited the Soviet Union, that the rural South should be seen as a "nation-within-a-nation." Harry Haywood, an African American who was the grandson of former slaves and a member of the Communist Party, pressed this point. Claude McKay, an émigré from Jamaica, promoted the idea of class from a racial point of view and offered an analysis that would prefigure Du Bois's *Black Reconstruction*.[13]

But the acceptance of the Black Belt thesis with its race-essential component would become the root of the white Left's messy entanglement with race for the remainder of the twentieth century. Despite the close rapport between many black intellectuals and the Left through literary and political activism, there continues to be a question of whether there was ever granted a full measure of independent thinking to the black intelligentsia. The Black Belt thesis offers an apt example of how a politics of identity and racial authenticity was constructed by the white Left with the aid of black radicals. But the idea that the only real authentic black culture came out of the rural South constricted the diversity of the African American experience. It failed to consider black Americans born outside the South, as well as those Afro-Caribbeans who had migrated into the North and South.[14]

Demographics certainly underpinned much of the logic of the Black Belt thesis, as well as the relatively recent memory of slavery. While there was certainly much to be learned from the black rural folk of the South (Zora Neale Hurston sought the preservation of that aspect of black life), there was also the reality of the Great Migration and the effects that urbanization had in creating a different kind of black culture. What black Southerners culturally brought to the cities of the North, Midwest, and West melded with ethnic and other black diasporic elements to create a black urban culture that was no less authentic than the countryside left behind.

The celebration of this emerging black culture in the 1910s and '20s was a major part of the Harlem Renaissance. Black writers and thinkers such as Langston Hughes, Claude McKay, Jesse Redmon Fauset, Nella Larsen, Wallace Thurman, and Arna Bontemps aimed at showing a diversity among black people even as they were bound together by the fact of Jim Crow segregation and general racial discrimination.[15]

Politically, most of the Renaissance writers moved in Left circles during the Depression. Langston Hughes, Richard Wright, and a young protégé of Hughes and Wright, Ralph Ellison, stand out. Hughes's earnest mixing of black rural folk culture with the rising urban black culture and the American literary canon that included Harriet Beecher Stowe, Walt Whitman, and Mark Twain laid the basis for a new, more complex rendering of the American identity. By the late 1930s, when the Popular Front came about, Langston Hughes was poised to be one of the most influential African American writers in that movement. The foundation that he laid would stretch beyond the 1930s and into the Cold War. Hughes's major accomplishment was his creation of Jesse B. Semple (Simple). While Hughes's poetry, prose, and drama in the early 1930s has been cited as part of his "revolutionary" period, it wasn't until the mid-1930s, when the Popular Front embraced race and ethnicity as a means to fashion a different American identity, that Hughes brought the Simple stories into being.[16]

Created in the *Chicago Defender*, a black newspaper that was, like most African American newspapers, conservative and middle-class oriented, Hughes posited a double-edged sword: on the one side, Jesse B. Semple was an embodiment of black folk/street culture, a "bluesman" whose insights were consonant with working-class values in a decidedly black world. But Simple was also American. As James Smethurst puts it, "Thus Hughes uses Simple to make an intraracial (as opposed to an interracial) argument against a Eurocentric model of cultural value that enshrines dead or near dead white people at the expense of the culture of the majority of African Americans."[17]

While Hughes wrote in leftist publications—communist or independent—more than most African American writers and was highly influential, his contemporary, Richard Wright, whose membership in the Communist Party was a direct result of his wanting to hone his craft as a writer, emerged as a more robust chronicler of the black masses. As a Mississippian who knew extreme poverty and the harshness of

Jim Crow segregation, Wright migrated north to Chicago to preserve his sanity. Chicago opened up a new world for him as it did for other African American migrants. But Wright felt an intense need to write about his experiences and those of other blacks weighted down by racial discrimination. He was, as Arna Bontemps put it, "a furious writer."[18]

But the ferocity of Richard Wright was, to put it bluntly, distorted by the cruel circumstances of his life. He never went to college like Langston Hughes, Ralph Ellison, or Margaret Walker but nonetheless was driven by the thirst for intellectual ideas to explain not only his craft but also the meaning of the African American experience. The Communist Party in Chicago, through its cultural support groups, afforded Wright the opportunity to grow intellectually.[19]

However, the calls for strict adherence to party doctrine continually collided with the independent vision of the artist. It was all well and good when Wright's prose and storytelling conformed to the proletarian struggles of working people who suffered under the oppressive weight of capitalism. And, of course, casting black culture within this frame- work met the accepted edict of the Black Belt thesis. But as the 1930s moved into the '40s and totalitarianism rose on the horizon, the pres- ence of Adolf Hitler and the tumultuous events in Josef Stalin's Soviet Union caused rifts in the American Communist Party's policies. The Nazi-Soviet Pact of 1939 concluded the dizzying shifts in party policy in the United States, with one of the results being a downplaying of race as a pressing concern. Among black intellectuals it created divisions similar to those experienced by white intellectuals. Wright, Hughes, and Ellison were mostly quiet. Hughes and Wright had championed the blacks who volunteered for the Abraham Lincoln Brigades that fought with the Spanish Republic against Francisco Franco, who was supported by the Fascists. There was similar support for Haile Selassie's defiance against Italy's attack on Ethiopia in the mid-1930s. And in the popular culture there was a swelling of pride when Jesse Owens upset Aryan notions of athletic superiority by taking home four Gold medals at the 1936 Olympics and Joe Louis knocked out Nazi-sponsored Max Schmeling in 1938.[20] Though there was a continuation of support for the Left's promotion of social justice and racial equality, many black intellectuals found themselves more in tune with the majority of Afri- can Americans when it came to any revolutionary changes suggested by the Communist Party. James Weldon Johnson, in the closing pages of his autobiography *Along This Way,* presented the best example of a liberal black intellectual stance on Communism. Johnson noted that "a restless fringe in the cities" might opt for Communism, but the African American community as a whole "shows practically no inclination to do so, either among the intellectuals or the masses."[21] Johnson advanced an argument that had been played out in the *Crisis* in the early 1930s when Du Bois wrote an editorial on the Negro and Communism. As Johnson put it,

> There are no indications that the United States will ever adopt Communism, and it is more than probable that in this country it will, in its present form, continue to be an outlawed political and economic creed; then for the Negro to take on the antagonisms that center against it, in addition to those he already carries would from any point of view, except that of fanaticism, be sheer idiocy. I feel the Negro should not hesitate at revolution that would bring in an era which fully included him in the general good, but, despite the enticing gestures being made, I see absolutely no guarantees that Communism, even if it could win, would usher in such an era.[22]

This summarized what would be the standard response of liberal black intellectuals with regard to Left politics in America for the remainder of the twentieth century. There was the hope for an integration of black Americans into the general society; a standard trope of all civil rights organizations then and now. There were also generational differences that divided African American thinkers like James Weldon Johnson, W. E. B. Du Bois, and the more conservative Kelly Miller from younger academic African Americans such as E. Franklin Frazier, Abram Harris, and Ralph Bunche and literary thinkers such as Richard Wright, Langston Hughes, and Margaret Walker.[23]

Finally there was a move above the wrangling and bitter feelings toward the Communist Party's tactics in the famed Scottsboro case. The NAACP and Du Bois felt that the Communist Party used the tragic incident of nine young black men accused by two white women of rape and sentenced to death as a means of recruiting black people into the party. The Communists condemned the NAACP as tools of the capitalist class. Of course, it did not help that the NAACP moved slowly in its response to the case. Once the Communist Party took on the case and organized rallies that brought the boys' relatives to Harlem and other cities, however, the NAACP was moved to orchestrate its own response, which largely consisted of questioning the sincerity of the Communists. For Du Bois, who did not believe that an alliance of black and white workers could overthrow the oppressor class, the Communist Party was woefully ignorant of black culture and southern black culture in particular. In his 1931 *Crisis* editorial "The Negro and Communism," he fumed, "American Negroes do not propose to be the shock troops of the Communist revolution, driven in the front to death, cruelty, and humiliation in order to win victories for white workers. . . . Negroes know perfectly well that whenever they try to lead revolution in America, the nation will unite as one fist and crush them and them alone."[24]

It was the prevailing racial discrimination and prejudicial mentality that was uppermost in Du Bois's mind. And yet, by 1934, after the Second Amenia Conference and before the publication of the Marxist-influenced historical study *Black Reconstruction*, Du Bois would be joining those young academicians such as Harris and Bunch and black literary figures such as Wright, Ellison, and Hughes in a criticism of the NAACP's overemphasis on integration in a time of great economic distress for African Americans. Immersing himself in Marx and reaching out to members of the Left both black and white, Du Bois exercised serious intellectual engagement in trying to resolve the economic and racial crises facing black America. The result was a seismic controversy that not only led to Du Bois's departure from the NAACP but also bequeathed a conundrum for black intellectuals to this day.

Thus James Weldon Johnson's appraisal of African Americans and Communism and the Left in general was more at the center of thinking among African American intellectuals. However much black intellectuals praised the antiracist stance of the Communists, most hesitated to fully embrace the party. There were certainly well-known black intellectuals who were either members of the Party or stalwart defenders. Many of these individuals were Afro-Caribbeans who adopted America as their new home but who also had an acute sense of the interplay of race and class in creating inequality, as well as strong black nationalist leanings. Cyrill Briggs, Otto Huiswood, and others had formed the African Blood Brotherhood in the 1920s as a means of fighting for civil rights and promoting racial pride. By the end of the 1920s, most if not all of its members joined the Communist Party.[25]

Many of the younger black intellectuals who leaned to the left and were sharply critical of civil rights organizations such as the NAACP and the National Urban League embraced the social science ideas that were emerging in the major universities of the nation. For sociologist E. Franklin Frazier, that meant training in the ideas expounded by Robert Park at the University of Chicago. Park's theory of race relations cycles that ended in assimilation greatly appealed to Frazier in at least two ways: it moved beyond race and racial essentialism and it comported well with a class analysis.[26]

Frazier's sociological work was centered on the black family, but he also studied the black middle class. What he found there disturbed him. In an article published in 1929 titled "Le Bourgeoisie Noir," which presaged his lengthier study in the late 1950s, Frazier noted, "Negro schools in the South furnish an example of the influence of middle class ideals which makes Negroes appear in a ridiculous light." Frazier also pointed out that "Negro newspapers are a good index of the extent to which middle class ideals have captured the imagination of Negroes."[27]

Because he had taught in black universities (Fisk and, in the 1930s, Howard), Frazier could knowledgably make these observations. "Le Bourgeoisie Noir" was a more balanced view of E. Franklin Frazier's conception of the black middle class. Nonetheless, it contained the essence of what would be a harsh and bitterly caustic assessment in the book *Black Bourgeoisie*, published just before Frazier's death.[28]

As a highly influential black sociologist, white intellectual America listened to Frazier's commentary. What was most striking was the attention paid to Frazier's belief that African Americans were Americans at the core. Slavery had acted as an eraser of any cultural affinity black people may have had with Africa. The black family, which Frazier focused on in his sociological work and which would influence national policy in later years, was severely disrupted by slavery. But as emancipation and education came to the Negro, improvement could be discerned. Thus in "Le Bourgeoisie Noir," Frazier asserted, "The first mistake of those who think that the Negro of all groups in America should be in revolt against the present system is that they regard the Negro group as homogeneous. As a matter of fact, the Negro group is highly differentiated, with about the same range of interests as the whites."[29]

For Frazier, the only hope of true radical change would come from an alliance between black and white workers. Yet he cautioned, "The Negro can only envisage those things that have meaning for him. *The radical doctrines appeal chiefly to the industrial workers, and the Negro has only begun to enter industry.*"[30]

Despite E. Franklin Frazier's leftward belief in interracial class alliance, his ideas were rooted in Robert E. Park's conservative but optimistic belief that society could be organized biracially. In Park's view (but not necessarily Frazier's), the "separate but equal" doctrine coupled with Booker T. Washington's model of industrial education (Park had worked with Washington at Tuskegee Institute for a number of years) had, by the early 1930s, reached a stage where African Americans were benefiting from imposed segregation. Thus Frazier could write suggestively in 1929 that in the black community "class differentiation among Negroes is reflected in their church organizations, educational institutions, private clubs, and the whole range of social life."[31] But Frazier was also a fervent opponent of segregation and went out of his way to push against those barriers publicly. He envisioned an integrated society where black people would reduce race to such a degree that it would be meaningless when set against their accomplishments economically and nationally as American citizens.[32]

Though there were hints that Frazier harbored some yearning for a black identity in terms of ethnicity, throughout most of his intellectual life, he battled against ideas of race essentialism and black nationalism. He dismissed the New Negro movement, stating, "The New Negro group which has shown a new orientation towards Negro life has restricted itself to the purely cultural in the narrow sense." These ideas set him in firm opposition with the emerging school of thought in the social sciences that saw culture and cultural behavior as a different, and more positively, defining light.

It is here that we must take note of the transformation of cultural anthropology through the work of Franz Boas. Throughout the 1920s, Boas worked to refute the central idea that races could be classified physically and that certain races (Native Americans and Africans) had inferior cultures or none worth noting. Boas put forth an idea that would become a centerpiece for the Left to approach race and culture. For Franz Boas, African Americans were hampered by the oppressive conditions experienced for generations and not by some inherent inability.[33]

As a German Jew who was raised in a liberal home devoted to Enlightenment ideals, Boas had experienced anti-Semitism. But when he settled in the United States and began to study the conditions under which African Americans lived, he was moved to comment, "The Negro of our times carries ever more heavily the burden of his racial descent than did the Jew of an earlier period; and the intellectual and moral qualities required to insure success to the Negro are infinitely greater than those demanded from the white, and will be greater, the stricter the segregation of the Negro community" (V. Williams, 25). But the core of Boas's thought and what endeared him to African American intellectuals in the early part of the twentieth century was his belief that no one culture was better than another. Each culture had something worthy and positive to offer humankind. This cultural relativism, however, was predicated on the idea that races or ethnic groups had particular identifiable traits that constituted not only an identity but a culture. For black Americans, that meant an identity that connected with Africa.[34]

This was where Boas was embraced, uncritically, by black intellectuals such as W. E. B. Du Bois, Carter G. Woodson, and sociologist Monroe Work. But there was a paradox to Boas's formulation: in his attempt to refute pseudo-scientific racist theories about blacks, he accepted the prevailing racialist assumptions of the day. Even as Boas regarded himself as an empiricist who concluded that the empirical data (in this case the cranial studies of races) did not support inferiority based on racial differences, his fervent belief in Enlightenment ideals of democracy and equality coupled with an acceptance of racial essentialist ideas put his notion of cultural relativism in a contradictory stance. In later years, when the culture wars would rage, conservative thinkers would attack this idea of cultural relativism, and Boas, for creating a situation where there would be a "ghettoization" or "balkanization" of races and ethnic groups in a "multicultural society" instead of a color-blind common culture.[35]

But the later conservative critique was only half right. Boas, like any intellectual of his times, could not escape certain racist anthropological assumptions, and with the rise of Nazism and its racist Aryan doctrine, Boas's commitment to cultural relativism was probably the most humane alternative. Furthermore, Boas believed that if African Americans could resolve their group identity situation they would be able to assimilate into American society.[36] This comported well with race men and women such as Du Bois, Woodson, Ida B. Wells-Barnett, and Anna Julia Cooper. But Boas was even more influential on a younger group of scholars and intellectuals who took up the idea of cultural relativism and its achievements.

During his tenure at Columbia University, Boas assembled a coterie of students and was able to test his ideas about cultures. Earlier in his career, he had waged a lonely and unsuccessful battle as a white man refuting racist ideas propagated by eugenicists such as Madison Grant and Lothrop Stoddard. These men advanced ideas about the demise of the civilized Nordic race due to cultural pollution through increased immigration from southern and eastern Europe. Grant in particular was instrumental in shutting off immigration in the 1920s. By the late 1920s and '30s, however, Boas was able to demonstrate empirically the fallacy and viciousness of these ideas.[37]

The challenge to the dominant view on race emanated mostly from the Left and contained some of the paradoxical formulations of Boas's thought. Boas's students Melville Herskovits and Zora Neale Hurston, and University of Chicago–trained Oliver C. Cox, set out to study, respectively, African American culture and its retentions; African American folk culture; and race, caste, and class in America.[38]

Politically, these intellectuals were not always on the same wavelength. Herskovits was clearly antiracist and a fervent believer in the cultural relativism that Boas advocated. His argument that African Americans held vestiges of their African past in terms of music, dance, and communal relations was challenged by the more class-oriented views of E. Franklin Frazier. The classic debate between Frazier and Herskovits has to be seen in the light of the Depression and the younger black intellectuals' attempt to move beyond race and challenge the systemic structures that caused racial discrimination and kept black Americans from advancing themselves into the mainstream of the American political economy. That meant that black people in America were Americans first and foremost who were denied their rights due to centuries of slavery and a betrayal of the promises of emancipation in Reconstruction. Cultural retentions that held links to Africa were nonexistent or mired in the race essentialism attached to nineteenth-century nationalist ideals.[39]

Herskovits and Frazier both believed in equality and democracy for African Americans. The division came over the question of culture. For Frazier, African Americans did not have a distinct culture but were rather part of the American culture as a whole. The removal from Africa and the many years of enslavement had erased any vestiges or carryovers from Africa. Black Americans assimilated European values and culture. Moreover, there was a strong blow to familial relations, which led to an inability to form healthy nuclear families. Frazier's ideas, promulgated in his books and articles, were very influential not only in the 1930s but throughout most of the twentieth century.[40]

Jonathan Scott Holloway's assessment of the Frazier-Herskovits debate reveals a traditional rendering: "This dilemma," Holloway states, "wrestling as it did with the issues of the value of European versus African cultures and with issues of racial capacity and ability to succeed, was at the very heart of the debate between Frazier and Herskovits. Thus the debate was not so much about how culture can survive catastrophic human traumas as it was about two things: blacks' ability to assimilate into the white majority and the terms through which this assimilation would operate."[41]

This traditional interpretation overlooks another way in which the Frazier-Herskovits debate could be understood. It could also be seen as being about cultural survival as well as about damage to black psyches (the pathological arguments in Frazier's thesis). Assimilation then becomes not only a question of African American capabilities but also the willingness of the white majority to accept into the mainstream a people who have been "damaged" by slavery. Liberals and many on the left would use this argument for pity as a moral instrument to prod the society into granting blacks equality and civil rights.[42]

Other proponents of Boas's cultural relativism were not as involved with the Frazier-Herskovits debate. Zora Neale Hurston saw Southern black folk culture as a dying artifact that needed preservation. The oral tales and folk customs, in Hurston's mind, were part of the United States and not just a separate reservoir of African retentions. Because she grew up surrounded by black people and somewhat sheltered from Jim Crow segregation (as well as having a vivid imagination), Hurston rarely put things in a racial context.[43]

Hurston may well have embraced "Papa Franz's" ideas about cultural relativism, but she did so only to show individual achievement. If the Negro people of the South had a rich folk culture, it owed more to the region and the material conditions of their lives than to their race. Hurston's idiosyncratic life and her conservative views regarding race often irked those African American intellectuals she associated with. They were certainly uncomfortable with her labeling the Harlem Renaissance crowd the "Niggerati" or the dialect-filled jokes and tales of Southern black folk she would relate at parties. But Hurston proved one thing that would be a common feature among black intellectuals, and that was a strong tendency to distance themselves from and, consequently, abstract the black masses. Hurston had an ability to see black people as individuals with all the foibles and virtues that human beings have. This is clearly seen in the chapter she excised from her autobiography, "My People, My People." Hurston was unafraid to critically lambaste black leadership, elites, or the masses. And yet there was certain warmth to the criticism. There was, it might be said, a love of black people that was not racially based but grounded in the simple acceptance of their humanity. In later years, Hurston's biting wit and her insights would influence writers such as Alice Walker (who brought

Hurston out of obscurity in the 1980s) and entertainers such as Chris Rock and Cedric the Entertainer.[44]

The diversity of Franz Boas's students was and continues to be a strong testimony to the viability of the cultural relativism that he propounded. If Herskovits took an Afrocentric approach and Hurston a more individualistic tack, Oliver C. Cox went further to the left and put forth an argument that melded caste, class, and race through a Marxian lens. Cox, curiously, has not received the attention he so richly deserves. Cox, an Afro-Caribbean like his contemporary Hubert Harrison, added a fresh perspective to the American racial dilemma that was progressive and internationalist in scope. Though he was on the left and was identified as a Marxist scholar, Cox never really affiliated with any political party or activist groups like Abram Harris, E. Franklin Frazier, or W. E. B. Du Bois did in the 1930s and '40s. His ideas, however, fit comfortably with the Popular Front in the 1930s, during the war years, and afterwards.[45]

Cox toiled away teaching at black colleges in the South, Tuskegee Institute in particular, and writing scholarly pieces for periodicals such as the *Journal of Negro Education*. Again, Cox's career was not unlike that of many young black intellectuals in the 1930s save for his immigration to the United States and his particular theories. Cox's theories on race and class not only challenged the dominant views of the time, they were in many ways the basis for our thinking about race and class relations in the late twentieth and early twenty-first centuries.

Oliver Cromwell Cox was born in Port of Spain, Trinidad, on 24 August 1901. His family, while large, was economically stable amid much Trinidadian impoverishment. Though the island was under British colonial rule, blacks were the majority population. Therefore, Cox did not experience a racial segregation that was violently enforced, as many African Americans did. There was discrimination based on color, class, and status, however (McAuley, 10–11). Cox's father encouraged and demanded the best from his children. A firm believer in the value of education, he encouraged all of his children, but especially his sons, to go to the United States to advance themselves educationally and careerwise. Cox came to America when he was eighteen, and at age nineteen, he attended the Central YMCA High School in Chicago to prepare himself for college. Upon graduation in 1923, he spent two years at the Lewis Institute majoring in history and economics. After receiving an associate's degree, Cox entered Northwestern University to study law and was granted a bachelor of science in law in 1929.

His expectations to return to Trinidad and practice law were dashed when he contracted polio. After spending a year and a half recovering, Cox decided to remain in academe. In 1930, he entered the economics department of the University of Chicago where he received a master's degree in 1932. It was at the University of Chicago that Cox developed the analytical skills that he would put to use in his later sociological work. His switch to sociology came because of his dissatisfaction with his teachers' inability to explain the causes of the Great Depression. He enrolled in the now-famed Chicago school of sociology (McAuley, 32–38).

However, Cox, unlike most of the black students studying there at the time, gravitated more toward quantitative work that involved case study and ecological methodology. Writing his dissertation on marital patterns among African Americans in the United States, Cox received the doctorate from Chicago two days after his birthday in 1938. In the dissertation, Cox made use of the quantitative methods he acquired under the training of William Ogburn and Samuel Stouffer. He also made use of the historical approach adopted by Louis Wirth regarding social problems and institutions. This training and the resulting dissertation would be put to brilliant use ten years later (McAuley, 39, 54).

But like almost all black intellectuals in this period, Oliver C. Cox was unable to get a position in a white university. He taught at Wiley College, a small black institution, in Marshall, Texas, for five years before moving on to a better position at Tuskegee Institute. Despite the advantage of a more lucrative position, Cox grew frustrated with the college's vocational mission. In 1949, Cox went to Lincoln University, where he spent most of his academic career (McAuley, 54–65).

In 1948, three years after the end of World War II, four years after the publication of the Swedish economist/sociologist Gunnar Myrdal's classic study of race relations in America, *An American Dilemma*, and on the cusp of the beginnings of a rabid anticommunist hysteria, Oliver C. Cox published *Caste, Class, and Race: A Study in Social Dynamics*. The book was not only the culmination of Cox's career but also a groundbreaking study in terms of providing a solid analytical framework for understanding how race and class were intertwined and embedded in American society. Cox's use of Marxian theory was not, as some critics claimed, overly deterministic and did not hew closely to a Communist line. Indeed, for Cox, Marxism was an explanatory tool arrived at after careful consideration of other paradigms (McAuley, chapter 3).

Like his contemporaries at the University of Chicago and most of the new breed of black social scientists that held sway in the 1930s, Oliver C. Cox was a strong believer in the objective scientific methodology. Like Abram Harris, E. Franklin Frazier, Ralph Bunche, Carter G. Woodson, Lorenzo Johnston Greene, Rayford Logan, and Charles Spurgeon Johnson, he was not an advocate of race essentialism. Like these intellectuals, Cox strongly believed that the problems of African Americans would end through assimilation or full integration into American society. But unlike his contemporaries, Cox remained, however much an independent thinker, firmly on the left. Harris had moved to the right by the end of the 1930s and embraced the values of marketplace capitalism. Frazier, despite attaining considerable recognition for his work and achievements in the field of sociology, was cynical and embittered at the end of his career over the state of black Americans. Frazier's last work, *Black Bourgeoisie,* bore this out and represented a thorough disdain with the progress of African Americans in the middle class. Frazier, too, had backed away from the radicalism of his youth. His studies of the black family and the cycle of social pathology due to socioeconomic disruption and a matriarchal family structure would influence public policy and African American intellectual discourse for the remainder of the twentieth century and into the twenty-first. Woodson and Greene were in the forefront of making African American history a rigorous, professionalized field that took up social science methodologies to challenge the pervasive racist interpretations of blacks in mainstream American history. Logan was one of the many who followed Woodson and Greene in this new history, and yet Logan, like most of those mentioned, was in the end a staunch integrationist who believed that African Americans should be full integrated in the American society.[46]

Oliver C. Cox, steadfast in his analytical rigor, author of three carefully researched and argued books on the historical origins of capitalism that predated scholarship on world systems and theories of uneven development of capitalism globally, was marginalized mostly because of the intense anticommunist climate of the late 1940s and '50s. The publisher of *Caste, Class, and Race,* Doubleday, let the first edition run out, rendering it out of print in 1949. It would be ten years later that a small independent leftist publishing house, Monthly Review Press, run by Marxist economist Paul Sweezy, would reprint Cox's book. By that time, though, the harshness of anticommunist actions such as the blacklists had abated, the Cold War mentality was being jarred by the Civil Rights movement, and Marxism was beginning to gain acceptance, and even respect, as an analytical tool in academe. But ever the independent thinker, Cox continued his work using Marxian theory while unafraid to critique certain aspects of Karl Marx's ideas (McAuley, 58–67).

Most intellectuals change their minds over the course of their lives. The reasons for doing so are so varied that it would take volumes to delineate them all. But in general, some cogent reasons have to do with their personality; the socioeconomic circumstances under which they evolved; the political climate, which can sometimes exert undue pressure; and the shift in the ways that they approach or apply ideas. There are few genuinely original thinkers in human history, as well as in African American history. W. E. B. Du Bois fits the mold as an original thinker who changed his mind many times over the course of his intellectual career. Alain Locke, who pursued philosophy with an end toward understanding African American art and being, can also be considered an original thinker in regard to the humanities. But within the social sciences, while there were and continue to be brilliant minds among African American scholars, Oliver C. Cox stands out, along with Du Bois, as an original thinker.[47]

The critical difference was that Du Bois was also a preeminent public intellectual who constantly spoke out on issues regarding black people nationally and colored peoples globally. Du Bois wrote widely and deeply whether as editor of the *Crisis* and other Afro-American papers and as author of essay collections, novels, and scholarly works. Du Bois, ever the activist, also ran for political office.[48] Other black scholars, intellectuals, and activists, whether they agreed with Du Bois or disagreed with him, nonetheless recognized the immense presence and influence that Du Bois wielded in the black world.

But Oliver Cromwell Cox operated in an entirely different manner. Cox spoke at scholarly conferences to predominately black audiences. He published works that were extensively researched but mostly placed in black journals. Cox did not publicly advocate or belong to any particular political party. Even though others labeled him a "Marxist sociologist," Cox did not identify himself as such. As much as he was on the left and as much as his intellectual work was driven by a profound belief in integration, Cox remained open-minded and alert to alternatives to his thinking. This independence would not sit well in the 1960s and early '70s when, as a visiting professor at Wayne State University, he conducted a graduate seminar on the development of capitalism that enraged a few black Marxist students in the course. Similar to experiences that Ralph Ellison, another independent Popular Front leftist, faced, Cox was called a "traitor" and an "Uncle Tom." Unfortunately, the subtle nuances of both Cox and Ellison's thinking were lost on the militant race- and class-conscious young people of that period.[49]

Oliver C. Cox, like Du Bois, Ralph Ellison, Zora Neale Hurston, Langston Hughes, and Richard Wright, to name but a very few, lived to see the emergence of the Civil Rights movement. Some were burned by the heat of the anticommunist fires that emanated from the government; others slid into the margins of obscurity and yet others, notably Richard Wright and the novelist Chester Himes, left the United States for Europe. Du Bois himself would leave for Africa where he would die on the eve of the March on Washington.

The class-driven ideas of the young black intellectual Turks of the 1930s receded only because of an overwhelming effort on the part of the nation's intellectual elite to present a consensus on the American culture. The ideas of class and race, however, remained in the background waiting to be heard again. For a new generation of African American intellectuals, the struggle for civil rights and social justice was proceeding energetically. Grassroots organizing, the idealism of youth who demanded their rights, and an economic prosperity came together to create a frisson that would dramatically redefine who and what an American was. It was the beginning of a time when the cloak of invisibility of African American intellectuals would be shed once and for all.

2

BLACK
INTELLECTUALS
AND THE QUEST
FOR LEGITIMACY:
CIVIL RIGHTS,
BLACK POWER,
AND THE
EXPENDITURE OF
MORAL CAPITAL

Amerida was in the midst of war. Nazi Germany's expansionist takeover of Europe, the attack on Pearl Harbor
by an equally expansionist Japan in the East, and the fascist government
of Italy that in the 1930s had attacked Ethiopia made for a triumvirate that seriously threatened civilization and world peace. While the
United States reacted strongly to the December 1941 attack by Japan,
the declaration of war on Germany and the rest of the Axis powers
might almost have seemed an afterthought.

From the perspective of many African American intellectuals, World
War II was a war about race, colonialism, segregation, and the possibilities for liberation from these forms of oppression. Adolf Hitler's
Aryan ideology displayed in every way possible a contempt of African-
descended people and Jewish people. The systematic plan for Germany
to expand in order to have *lebensraum* (living space) for its people led
to the willful policy of mass extermination of Jews and represented
the horrific logical conclusion of eugenics and statist racism. It was no
wonder that most African American intellectuals and political leaders
ultimately endorsed the "double V": victory over Germany and victory
over segregation at home.[1]

And yet for many African American intellectuals, the response to
Japan was more complex. Japan, before Pearl Harbor and as far back
as the early years of the twentieth century, had represented something

more positive: a people of color who, as a nation, had marshaled strength and assertiveness to match almost anything that the West had produced. Overlooked by many was the fact that Japan harbored some vile racist attitudes of their own toward Koreans and Chinese peoples. Their belief in their own supremacy saw them at the top of the Asian peoples and was not unlike the way that the British saw themselves vis-à-vis other European nations.[2]

Because Japan, unlike Germany, made some overtures to black Americans and because in certain sectors of black America there was a strong belief in an Afro-Asiatic connection, black intellectuals appeared willing to, long before America's entry into war, to give Japan some benefit of the doubt. However, the responses after the United States began gearing up for the war were for the most part mixed.[3]

Japanese propaganda to African America was intense during the 1930s and for the most part well received. Tinged with a racialism that appealed to a black nationalism that hungered for a model of fortitude and self-respect, Japan represented a nation that stood apart from and yet saw itself equal to any of the Western powers but the British Empire in particular. In the United States, Japanese envoys such as Hikida Yasuichi, Naka Nakene, a Japanese activist, and Masao Dodo, a Japanese journalist, among others, spoke at black rallies and lived in black communities to point out racial affinity and solidarity.[4]

On the West Coast, African American newspapers such as the *California Eagle* were, for the most part, pro-Japan. There was an attempt on the part of the black press in this region to portray Japanese people as a group that black people should emulate. Even on the East Coast, the sentiment of group solidarity rang out in Harlem's *Amsterdam News*. Just about the only black sector of reservation regarding Japan came from the Left.[5]

African American intellectuals and political activists, whether in the Communist Party, sympathetic to the Party, or who otherwise held progressive beliefs, saw the Japanese as one of the Axis powers, whose ideology rested on a virulent racism. As difficult as it may have been to go against what many black Americans have felt about Japan and a supposed "Afro-Asiatic connection," Japan's imperialist designs and racial supremacist views were unacceptable. On the West Coast, the black Left watched the Japanese propaganda movement in the black community as closely as the FBI did. What they saw made them very concerned. But matters would become even murkier as events in Europe unfolded in the late 1930s and early '40s.[6]

33

Hitler's nonaggression pact with Josef Stalin's Soviet Union caused the American Left to align with the Popular Front, which denounced the West's imperialist approach. Here was a strong push for democracy at home and a hands-off stance regarding foreign affairs. In a peculiar way this dovetailed with a general feeling of isolationism in the nation. But the crucial difference was that along with foreign policy, the Left sought to change the way the government treated minorities, workers, and the poor.[7]

The Popular Front that emerged was a transformative force in American culture. African American intellectuals such as Richard Wright, Langston Hughes, and Ralph Ellison moved in these progressive circles and were able to hone their talents and make an imprint. The key effect of these three writers/thinkers was in how they situated race in the American scheme. Much like the African American historians who sought to recover and vindicate black Americans in American history, Wright, Hughes, and Ellison strove to show how American culture, indeed the American experience, rested on a foundation of blackness.[8]

That's why the black masses' fascination with Japan, stoked by an otherwise middle-class-oriented and conservative black press, placed these writers on the fringe. Richard Wright recalled how his grandmother had spoken highly of Japanese people when he was little. As a Communist, however, Wright was more suspicious of Japanese intentions. Langston Hughes had a bitter experience in his travels when he encountered Japanese discrimination.[9] For W. E. B. Du Bois, the master of double consciousness, the lure of Japan was even more complex. As an internationalist who placed a great deal of faith in the solidarity of the colored peoples of the world, Du Bois saw Japan as an example of a strong united nation that could not only stand up to Western powers but also provide a model for other nations of color, particularly in Africa, to emulate. As ever, Du Bois walked a tightrope that had him admiring the racial achievements of a nation such as Japan while warily supporting the progressive causes of the Popular Front.[10]

It was most distressing to many African American intellectuals on the left when Hitler broke his pact with the Soviet Union and attacked that nation in 1941. The American Communist Party, following the Comintern, did an about-face and called for a "people's war for democracy." The Popular Front's attention to transforming American culture halted as the Left encouraged blacks and workers to gear up for war. Such a turnabout was too much for Richard Wright, who, although he had remained in the Communist Party, had experienced increasing tensions over his artistic views. For Wright, the party had offered him a vision of what integration could mean. But increasingly, he came to see how poor blacks were being exploited to suit party interests. The new turn toward joining with the West and Russia against Hitler caused an irreparable break with the party for Wright.[11]

Ralph Ellison was also concerned. He did not approve of a war in Europe and did not want to fight in a segregated army. In the end, he would join the Coast Guard. Langston Hughes took another tack: he supported the war effort. This put him in alliance with the *Pittsburgh Courier*'s slogan "double V" for victory.[12]

What placed these black thinkers and other African Americans in a bind over supporting the war was the continuing pervasiveness of Jim Crow segregation in the United States. While lynching had abated, there was still the fact that African Americans faced police brutality in urban centers, discrimination in access to meaningful employment, and, even more galling, discrimination in the defense industries and the armed forces. It was the last of these that set up a divide between those African Americans who were ready to fight for their country and those who saw a racist nation unwilling to grant black people freedom but ready to crush a nation such as Japan.

While Richard Wright was fiercely anti-Nazi, he was unwilling to enter the armed forces to face harsh treatment in the Southern boot camps and a segregated troop assignment thereafter. Wright, however, had an out: he was at first classified 3A because he had a wife and new-born child and was taking care of his mother. When the classification was changed to 1A, Wright attempted to secure a position as a writer for the Office of War Information. He also sought to be reclassified 3A. Wright was turned down for any writing or reportorial position in the armed forces but was reclassified 3A. No reasons were given for the rejection and we are left to speculate as to why he was not accepted. It may well be that as a highly visible black man for his time—author of a well-known novel, member of the Communist Party, and outspoken on race issues—Wright was too much for the government. But therein lies the dilemma: in fighting a war against nations that were actively promoting racism, the United States could not afford to come off looking two-faced on the matter of racial discrimination.[13]

As black men from across the country trained for war in boot camps in the segregated South and faced the racist mores of that region, other African Americans were being denied employment in defense plants. By 1943, black American anger had boiled over: riots began springing up in the North, South, and West. And these occurred two years after the threat of a march on Washington, organized by A. Philip Randolph, had been averted by an executive order signed by President Franklin Delano Roosevelt barring discrimination in the defense industries. What seemed like a victory for the government inclusion of African Americans and a blow against discrimination, however, was in actuality a political compromise that tarnished Randolph's leadership and allowed the government to continue segregation in the armed forces. And little was done to correct the systemic racial prejudice that led to the frustration and anger among the masses of black Americans.[14]

Asa Philip Randolph, aided by a young pacifist, Bayard Rustin, had worked strenuously to rid the discrimination in the nation's defense industries. To his credit, Randolph pulled together in his "Negroes Committee to March on Washington for Equal Participation in National Defense" the various contending strands of black leadership and intellectual thought. Walter White of the NAACP was on board and represented the integrationist strain while Rayford Logan brought intellectual and historical acumen to the committee. Reverend Lloyd Ames was clearly representative of the black church.[15]

The manifesto calling for the march on Washington was forthright in its demands but also peculiarly structured so as to appease the various views of those African American leaders and thinkers. The threat of bringing hundreds of thousands of Negroes to the nation's capitol moved Roosevelt to act. Despite the compromise in Executive Order 8802, a precedent of sorts was set: threats of mass demonstration and appeals to the American creed would become building blocks toward the accumulation of moral capital for the procurement of African American civil rights. Other actions by African Americans and a groundbreaking study increased that acquisition.

The move toward mass demonstrations, like earlier efforts to boycott businesses, represented a mode of thinking in black communities that sought to fight racial discrimination and barricades to opportunities for meaningful work and an improved quality of life. Such demonstrations stressed that black people should be accorded the same treatment as whites. Indeed what many African Americans sought was a "blueprint for first class citizenship." Pauli Murray, writing of demonstrations for civil rights by Howard University students, noted, "The question remains to be settled during the coming months whether Howard students shall participate in social action directed against second-class citizenship to which they have been victimized."[16]

In 1944, as the war in Europe and the Pacific was beginning to turn toward victory, there appeared a massive study of the "Negro Problem" that had been four years in the making. The huge analysis of American race relations with an eye toward the amelioration, if not elimination, of racial prejudice was the result of white American philanthropy's desire to bring this perennial problem to a close. *An American Dilemma: The Negro Problem and Modern Democracy* by the Swedish economist and social democrat Gunnar Myrdal would become the chief document by which American liberalism would engineer the civil rights movement of the next generation.

Myrdal's study, which used the work and consultations of such black intellectuals as Ralph Bunche, Charles S. Johnson, Abram Harris, and E. Franklin Frazier, prided itself on its inclusion of black thinkers. Having spent a good deal of time traveling in the South speaking with thinkers such as Du Bois at Atlanta University, Monroe Work at Tuskegee Institute as well as the triumvirate—Harris, Frazier, and Bunche—at Howard University, Myrdal also spoke to sharecroppers and visited black bars, churches, and secondary schools. All of these currents of thinking centered on what was the best way to improve the condition of the Negro.[17]

And yet a study as vast and intense as this one was not headed by any African American (one thinks of Du Bois as the obvious choice). Even though black intellectuals had produced works on life and conditions—works that ranged from Du Bois's early Atlanta University studies of the Southern blacks to Horace Cayton and St. Clair Drake's later dynamic study of Bronzeville in Chicago in *Black Metropolis* (1945) or E. Franklin Frazier's incisive study of the 1935 Harlem race riot and later the black family—most white philanthropists held the idea that not only could black scholars not be objective in their studies but more importantly that they really had nothing original worth talking about. Thus, a cloak of invisibility was thrown over the ideas, however diverse and original, that African American intellectuals might put forward to enrich and deepen any discourse seeking to ameliorate race relations.[18]

But, then again, given the historical context, anything original that black intellectuals had to say most likely was going to interfere with the nation's attempt during wartime to remold itself into a unified liberal nationalist state. That reformulation was driven by efforts to put forward the ideology of the "Four Freedoms" and democracy as opposed to totalitarianism whether under the guise of Nazism, fascism, or communism. FDR's dictum of "no privileged people" presumably looked to equality and inclusiveness. For some black intellectuals, especially those who aided Gunnar Myrdal in his study, such as Bunche, Harris, and Frazier, this resonated with their belief in an integration of African Americans to where race would eventually disappear from the national discourse. As Nikhil Pal Singh aptly put it, "In contrast to a prior generation of leftists, as well as to a future generation of civil rights liberals for whom racial integration essentially meant the public invisibility of blacks as blacks, activist intellectuals such as [C. L. R.] James, [Richard] Wright, and [Ralph] Ellison refused to accept anything that smacked of submission to civic inferiority."[19]

Therefore Myrdal's study, however much it framed the agenda for liberals—black and white—on civil rights over the next two decades, still contained a contending though obscured set of concerns for those black intellectuals who were skeptical of *An American Dilemma*. These intellectuals harkened back to the 1930s when they developed social scientific studies that sought to expose the conditions of African Americans in as objective a manner as possible. Ideologically, these individuals traversed the spectrum from the moderate conservatism of Charles Spurgeon Johnson to the Marxist, later turned conservative Abram Harris to the left-leaning, then turned liberal integrationist Ralph Bunche and the iconoclastic radicalism of Oliver C. Cox. Even those African American intellectuals who were enamored of the organized Left with its presumed belief in racial equality—socially and politically—held to a firm notion that an African American nationalist experience was essential to the American enterprise. Integration for them, to use Singh's incisive words, "presumed neither political accommodation nor normative assimilation. Rather, it imagined the independent, democratic, self-mobilization of blacks as one of its prerequisites" (127–28).

Looked at from this angle, if the Myrdal study had allowed that set of ideas to be placed at its core rather than the reliance it took on an American creed founded on a moralistic pretext, the future course of race relations would have been vastly different. African American intellectuals could have been given not only legitimacy for their ideas but also visibility on an equal standing with other American intellectuals. In other words, black intellectuals would have had a clear voice in any discourse that might have maintained, reformed, or called for complete change of the sociopolitical order.[20]

Yet another way of ascertaining the impact of Myrdal's study on African American intellectual discourse can be found in Jonathan Scott Holloway's assessment. For Holloway, the 1930s generation of black intellectuals was transitional and their "work led to the legitimation of social science expertise on race relations through Gunnar Myrdal's *An American Dilemma* project, it broadened the scope of accepted intellectual of discourse by blacks, and it helped to enlarge the terrain of professional possibilities for black scholars."[21] In a nutshell, Myrdal's study laid the foundation for future black public intellectual discourse. A "black" world view as presented through the writings and activities of Richard Wright, Langston Hughes, Ralph Ellison, Ella Baker, Margaret Alexander Walker, and any others who moved among and listened closely to what the black masses were saying was not likely to be within the "scope of accepted intellectual discourse" that *An American Dilemma* allowed for. And while certainly the terrain for black professional opportunities would open up in future years, it would do so only under the aegis of a Cold War liberal anticommunism that felt the pressure to live up to the ideals of the New Deal American creed while also maintaining a market society that would ensure prosperity through consumption and exportation of American principles globally.[22]

Myrdal's study did not go without challenges, and it is instructive how the critiques of Myrdal have been deflected in such a manner as to cast off those who questioned the study to the margins of intellectual discourse. Such marginalization said much about how a true black intellectual critique was and continues to be received in the United States. The two main critiques of Myrdal came from Oliver C. Cox and Ralph Ellison. Cox's criticism was published in an academic journal and quickly attacked by one of Myrdal's consultants, E. Franklin Frazier. Cox aptly criticized the moralistic premises of the study and called for a more materialist class analysis.[23] The move to marginalize Cox's incisive critique owed much to Cox's being shut out by the University of Chicago's Robert Park's school of sociology scholars. Charles S. Johnson and E. Franklin Frazier were stalwart students of Robert Park. Park, in turn, was closely associated with Booker T. Washington and Tuskegee. Park's intricate schema for how race relations could be improved heavily bore the marks of Bookerite accommodationism even as its end conclusion was to result in the total assimilation of blacks into white society.[24]

Within constricted academic circles, Cox's critique was argued or dismissed and eventually pushed into obscurity as the nation moved into the postwar era that heralded a common culture consensus that pressed freedom and progress against an ominous communist threat of global takeover. To that end, Ralph Ellison's review of Gunnar Myrdal received a significant and even more telling response. Ellison prepared his critique for the *Antioch Review* in 1944. He was anxious for its appearance for he saw in Myrdal's project all the disadvantages that social science analyses could bestow on black Americans and their presence in America. The review was an elegant literary piece of writing. It started out in quiet measured tones and, almost jazzlike, rose the scales into a blistering criticism of Myrdal's work.[25] For Ellison, *An American Dilemma*, with its moralistic premise and its optimism in the liberal faith of reason and education as the tools to ameliorate race relations, robbed African Americans of their humanity. Black culture was emotional, irrational, rich and deep, and highly transformative of American culture. How could it not be given the particular historical experiences that black people had gone through in the nation's history? From Ellison's view, Myrdal completely missed the importance of black Americans' agency in American history. What angered Ellison most was that in 1,483 pages, black people were looked upon with liberal pity rather than understood as human beings who persevered through the trials and tribulations of slavery and created important institutions and cultural products within the stifling confines of Jim Crow segregation. The lack of historicity left Ellison cold toward the report.[26]

Ralph Ellison's review of *An American Dilemma* would not see the light of publication until he produced his first collection of essays, *Shadow and Act* in 1962. By then, Myrdal's work, however criticized by white intellectuals, was firmly planted as a cornerstone in the liberal struggle for civil rights. Ellison had written *Invisible Man* a decade earlier to great acclaim even as it was criticized by some on the left for lacking in protest. Nonetheless, liberals who embraced the Cold War ethos welcomed the novel. It would take conservatives at least another generation to appropriate Ellison (like Frederick Douglass and Martin Luther King Jr.) to their own ideological ends.[27]

Ellison's point was missed by all sides, and he would spend much of the rest of his intellectual career fighting for an artistic rendition of a nationalistic yet highly integral black culture in American society. Ellison wanted the United States to understand its miscegenated past even as it was splintered by racism, class divisions, regionalisms, and political faction. Black American culture in all of its diversity was part and parcel of an American culture that reinvented itself fluidly but also denied its essential historical identity. That denial not only caused pain and division but threatened, from Ellison's viewpoint, to erase the truly genuine and positive qualities of the country.[28]

Ellison's hopeful, some would say optimistic, view of blacks in America was conditioned in part by his historical experiences in the 1930s within the black world of the South, the integrated "territory" of Oklahoma, and his keen observations of the rise of an urban black culture where the rural Southern black mixed with the Northern black and the Afro-Caribbean immigrants. This heady brew was richly portrayed in *Invisible Man* as IM makes his journey from South to North and encounters various strata in the black and white worlds of the United States. *Invisible Man* becomes a serious intellectual compass for understanding what African Americans faced in mounting the drive for freedom in civil rights and human rights.[29]

Though Ellison operated from a leftist position throughout the 1930s and much of the '40s, his intense preoccupation with his novel, the separation from his friend Richard Wright, and the movement of mainstream civil rights organizations to embrace the anticommunism of Cold War liberalism left Ellison isolated. He was always conscious that his novel would weave the respected works of American literature with the rustic folk culture of black people. His friendship with Langston Hughes, his deep love of jazz, and his learned observations of urban black culture gained during his work with the Federal Writers Project gave Ellison enough tools for his creation. His deep friendship with Wright (whom he vigorously defended, on Marxian grounds no less, when Wright's *Native Son* was attacked by Communists) introduced Ellison to the French existentialists André Malraux, Jean-Paul Sartre, and Jean Genet. Ellison profited from these thinkers and other American writers such as Ernest Hemingway, Nathaniel Hawthorne, and his namesake, Ralph Waldo Emerson.[30]

The gravitas of *Invisible Man* elicited critically acclaimed reviews, awards, and an entrée into the world of letters for Ralph Ellison. But the price was to set him a distance from the black world that he really did love. Though he lived in Harlem with his second wife, Fanny, for the rest of his life and gave talks, in the grand tradition of black intellectuals, to black schools, churches, and community organizations, he also went to Europe on a generous grant and was offered visiting professorships at predominately white universities. Ellison became integrated into American intellectual society well before the massive movement of young black educators emerged in the 1980s.[31]

The path of Ralph Ellison's intellectual journey is a well-told one. But key moments occurred during the height of the Civil Rights–Black Power movements and into the 1980s, when the ascendancy of the Right threatened to roll back the achievements of the Civil Rights movement. In both cases, Ellison found himself under intense and painful scrutiny. The heat of the Civil Rights movement boiled over with frustration at the slow response of the federal government to the marches, demonstrations, and impassioned pleas of Southern blacks who were treated to fire hoses, police dogs, cattle prods, confinement to prisons (where they were often beaten), and death. By the time the Civil Rights Act of 1964 and the Voting Rights Act of 1965 were passed, the vision of a radicalized black nationalism loomed large.[32]

Ellison was certainly aware of the events swirling around him and supported what he called the "freedom struggle." He was in the midst of composing his next novel but had also published a book of essays that in any other time would have identified him with the independent Left. But in the glare of the Civil Rights movement, the essays seemed quaint or even cranky. Older black nationalist intellectuals such as John O. Killens and John Henrik Clarke found Ellison too individualistic and detached from black protest if not black culture in toto. His work seemed too fatalistic and unmotivating for a movement that had been taken over by young black and white college students. But it was the young nationalists (termed "black militants" by the media) in the new Black Power movement who unloaded their harshest criticism on Ellison.[33]

In an interview with James Alan McPherson, an emerging black writer who was clearly enamored of Ellison and devoted to his writings, Ellison spoke about the angry black youth and the trajectory of the movement. When confronted by black students at Oberlin in 1969, he was told bluntly that his work had no meaning for them. While Ellison accepted that criticism, he tried to explain that *Invisible Man*, written long ago, was one interpretive point of view. It was then that he was called an "Uncle Tom."[34]

McPherson noted that Ellison's harsh encounters were the result of "any black who attempts to assert his own individuality in his own terms . . . that challenges the defense mechanisms" resulting from the forced binding of a people who were once enslaved and never fully emancipated. The veil cast by Jim Crow segregation, whether overt in the South or covert in the North or West, had forced African Americans to create their own institutions and role models based on a "group-think" that never pushed too hard against the color line (McPherson, 359).

For black intellectuals like Ellison, Zora Neale Hurston, and countless others who presented alternative visions to the group understanding of blackness, the reaction could be swift and harsh. The criticism could range from outright dismissal as in the case of Hurston and most black women writers/thinkers (even in the 1980s and '90s, African American women struggled mightily to gain a voice and a hearing) to the accusation that black thinkers were trying "to be white" or "tomming" to curry favor with the white intelligentsia. There may well have been black thinkers who moved in that direction. But the African American intellectuals examined here, as much as that criticism was aimed at them or they were ignored, had profoundly important things to say to the race, for the race, and to American society in general.[35]

Ellison, for one, saw the United States as miscegenated. Black culture was absorbed into American life on almost every level. This insight by Ralph Ellison may seem trite today, but in the 1950s and '60s, it was a bombshell. That black culture is American culture and vice versa has become a commonplace notion in a society where hip-hop is culturally well into the mainstream, the most lucrative movie stars are black actors and actresses such as Denzel Washington, Will Smith, and Halle Berry, and the sports arenas from football to basketball to baseball to tennis to golf are richly painted in hues of black. However, to state the vision that Ellison portrayed in *Invisible Man* and more subtly in his posthumously published novel *Juneteenth* was jarring to an intellectual community and a nation that still saw America divided along a binary fault line of black and white.[36]

And there should be no mistaking that Ellison and his heirs, black writers such as James Alan McPherson, Cecil Brown, Ishmael Reed, Stanley Crouch, and Ellison's good friend Albert Murray in different variations, riffs if you will, played off Ellison's vision. Ellison never walked away from the black world as much as he tried to help black people see that they were integral in shaping not only whites' perceptions but also America's view of who they were.[37]

"A few people," Ellison said to McPherson in a 1970 interview, "can trace their connections back to a given African tribe, but most of us cannot. We can't even trace most of our blood back to Africa because most of us are part Indian, Spanish, Irish; part any and every damn thing. But *culturally* we represent a synthesis of any number of these elements, and that's a problem of abstraction in itself; its abstraction and recombining. Thus African Americans are intricately involved in the creative process of re-inventing and trans-forming themselves and America" (McPherson, 373).

The pinnacle of what Nikhil Pal Singh calls "the long civil rights movement," might be the *Brown v. Board of Education* decision in 1954 that struck down the notion of separate but equal education and, subsequently, other accommodations for blacks and whites. Given the fact that there were rare efforts to create separate but equal schools everywhere at all times, the Warren Court's decree was hailed as a breakthrough for social justice. Yet subsequent rulings left little doubt that white supremacy still reigned.

There has been no major revolution in modern history to occur without intellectuals; conversely there has been no major counterrevolutionary movement without them. Intellectuals have been the fathers and mothers of movements, and of course sons and daughters, even nephews and nieces.[38]

African American intellectuals by the end of the twentieth century faced a future full of challenges that could be uplifting and bountiful for all black people or continue a grim and devastating fissure between black haves and black have-nots. That widening of the socioeconomic gap most certainly would have a significant impact on the larger society. And as has so often happened in American history, those whites in power either moved cynically to alleviate the situation or were indifferent to critical needs in ways that were not likely to benefit black America. The key for black intellectuals was to replenish a diminished reservoir of moral capital and correct a steady movement among the black middle class into a romantic neosegregation in the face of assaults that had been made on the gains from the Civil Rights movement of decades ago.

That would be no simple task. For black intellectuals, despite enjoying a visibility unprecedented in American history, were farther removed from the masses of African Americans than at any other time in their history. With black America having successfully struggled to gain the legal rights to move socially in public accommodations and to exercise use of the ballot freely, there had been remarkable achievements that went beyond the progress and nadir of the Reconstruction and Redemption periods of the nineteenth century. The fact that the black middle class grew as large as it had and that black people were now deeply ensconced in the political system were but two significant accomplishments that indicated not only the demise of Jim Crow segregation but also the strength and moral acuity of black intellectual leadership and the actions of the black masses who inspired that leadership.

But not everything went as hoped. A new generation of African Americans emerged that knew the history of struggle only through documentaries such as Henry Hampton's *Eyes on the Prize* or from rap groups such as KRS-1 or Public Enemy, who attempted to resuscitate a feeling of pride and consciousness among black youth in general and inner-city youth living in dangerous environments in particular. Indeed, the more traditional black intellectuals of the present were hardly known by these young people; their constituency included those blacks and whites in academia or in certain areas of the political world.

Unable to make the connection either with the immiserated black poor or many of those newly arrived in the black middle class, black intellectuals found themselves visible but encapsulated in an insulated academic world that may listen but often does not hear and does not act on the ideas, analyses, and prescriptions that these women and men present. African American intellectuals of the late twentieth century had no real movement with which to energize the masses of African Americans and provide them with real hope for the future; rather, they continue to be marginalized in making an impact on major policy decisions. Only in the early twenty-first century would an African American politician, Barack Obama, emerge to galvanize the general population and inspire new hope. But Obama split African American intellectuals along the lines of multiculturalism and black traditionalism.

The loss of moral capital and the inability to fully address some of the ideas put forth by the twentieth century's more serious black intellectuals, such as W. E. B. Du Bois, Ralph Ellison, Michelle Wallace, Patricia Hill Collins, and bell hooks, created a critical impasse in any movement for social justice and advancement for African Americans and America in general.

Moral capital here means the resources accumulated from the historical experiences of African Americans from the time that they were forcibly brought to these shores to the moment when they successfully broke the chains of legal segregation and began to move into the light of freedom. Moral capital means that vast reservoir of knowledge, perseverance, and determination used by black women and men who struggled for freedom to be not just American but to be recognized and accepted as human beings whose accomplishments were as worthy and valuable as anyone else's. Finally moral capital addresses the historical sense of social justice that has evolved over the centuries that black people have been present in this land. This social justice is intimately tied to what this nation has conceived itself of as being and has fallen short of reaching. Thus the notion of social justice is not about "simple justice" but about seeking a transformation that involves a renewing, if not a rebuilding, of who Americans, black and white, are as a nation and as a people.

The loss of moral capital happened ironically enough when the Civil Rights revolution proved successful in its expansion and integration of the black middle class in American society. To understand that irony perhaps one must go back in time to the hope and promises of Reconstruction, which failed to deal with issues of race, class, and gender, and identify the sources of the Civil Rights movement.

In 1930, almost thirty years after the Supreme Court decision of *Plessy v. Ferguson* codified the foundation for Jim Crow segregation, black America found itself deeply mired in economic depression. Upwards of half the employable population was out of work. In cities such as Philadelphia, the unemployment rate reached 52 percent by 1932. This grim situation existed in most of the urban areas of the nation.[39] Despite the fact that significant numbers of African Americans had migrated in the previous twenty years to urban areas, the majority continued to reside in the South where the color line was strictly enforced. For black communities living under Jim Crow, there were few resources that they could call on to demonstrate that the meaning of "separate but equal" was a reality. Nonetheless, there were some institutions that gave succor to a people considered less than human by much of the nation's populace. These included the black church first and foremost, the various small businesses that catered to the needs of the community, and the public schools and black colleges.

It was the black colleges, particularly those that had been set up after the Civil War, that housed the black intellectual elite of African America. Most of these colleges and universities were started after the Civil War as a means of educating the emancipated slaves. Aided by church groups such as the American Missionary Association and later by philanthropic foundations, thousands of teachers came South to educate the freed people in the ways of citizenship, industry, and morality as well as the "three R's."

Black people themselves eager to learn participated in building their own schools. One of the major movements of Reconstruction among black legislators and their white allies was the creation of a common educational program for all of the people of the South.[40] But it was in the area of higher education that the production of black intellectuals would have a significant impact on African America. Many of the most prominently known figures in black history received their education or parts of it in black colleges that had been created after the Civil War. For example, W. E. B. Du Bois spent his undergraduate years at Fisk University and Booker T. Washington studied at Hampton Institute. But more importantly, most if not all of the important black intellectuals from the late nineteenth century to the beginning of the 1960s taught at black colleges or universities.

It would be a lengthy list indeed to name all of those black thinkers who populated the black colleges and universities from the late nineteenth to the mid-twentieth centuries. Even more tragic was the fact that many of those men and women were hardly known to a generation that views the years of the Civil Rights movement as ancient history. It is important to recall a few of those whose achievements have impacted on present-day American race relations.

One of the positive features of the visibility of black public intellectuals in the later twentieth century was the presence of African American women thinkers. Not that they were not present in the past. Indeed, because of black women's voices in the present, we have come to know and think about those intellectuals in earlier years who played important, if not always acknowledged, roles in uplifting the race, struggling for civil rights and women's equality. Foremost among these women was Anna Julia Cooper, who strenuously called for the formal education of black women. Although Cooper's thinking reflected many of the contradictions within racial uplift ideology, she was nonetheless a pioneering educator and thinker regarding the role that black women should play in the general uplift of the race. Kevin Gaines, who has masterfully analyzed Cooper's thought, is correct in noting, "The impulse to reclaim Cooper as a black feminist intellectual, although undoubtedly of value within an African American intelligentsia and U.S. political culture still resistant to gender equality, may ultimately impose artificial limits on the critical consideration Cooper warrants."[41]

This claim could be made for almost any of the black women thinkers of the past. The historical influences for bell hooks, Toni Morrison, Patricia Hill Collins, Hazel Carby, Hortense Spillers, Trudier Harris, Patricia Williams, and Michele Wallace to name but a few examples could be found in Cooper, Ida Wells-Barnett, Alice Dunbar-Nelson, Zora Neale Hurston, Fannie Barrier Willams, Jesse Fauset, Nannie Burroughs, and Mary Church Terrell. These black women intellectuals were very active within the constraints imposed by the gender conventions of their day. Their perseverance and critical observations added immeasurably to that fund of moral capital that sustained black people struggling for civil liberties and human dignity.[42]

Again, many of those women of the past were trained in or taught at black colleges. More importantly, despite their being members of an intellectual elite, they were never far removed from their black communities. In many cases, like their male brethren, they traveled throughout the country speaking in black communities at church gatherings or YWCAs. They were members of black women's organizations, the largest of which was the National Association of Colored Women, and writers for black newspapers.[43] However, society's gender constraints, with its insistence on women being guardians of morality within the home, muffled much of the more critical ideas that African American women had to offer. And in the 1930s it was black male intellectuals who were most often heard in the small public space that they held.

If Harvard University had a black counterpart in the 1930s it would most certainly have been Howard University. In the 1920s and into the Depression, Howard employed most of the leading black intellectuals in the country. Alain Leroy Locke in philosophy, E. Franklin Frazier and Kelly Miller in sociology, Rayford Logan, Lorenzo Greene, and Charles Wesley in history, Arna Bontemps and Arthur Davis in English, and the biologist Ernest E. Just. There was also Ralph Bunche in political science, James Naibrit in economics, William Hastie and Charles Houston in law.

These scholars were connected to the black communities of not only Washington, D.C., but also the rest of the nation's urban centers. They were also advisors to architects of Roosevelt's New Deal, contributors to the mammoth study of the "Negro Problem" undertaken by Gunnar Myrdal, and ultimately teachers of those who would be active in the Civil Rights movement.[44] Many were in touch with those African American public intellectuals who did not hold academic posts. These personages were often literary figures or political activists who expressed their views in black newspapers or black organizational organs such as the NAACP's *The Crisis* or the National Urban League's *Opportunity*. Again the list of these individuals is lengthy, but some are noteworthy: Langston Hughes, George Schuyler, Hubert Harrison, A. Philip Randolph, John Davis, Arthur A. Schomburg, J. Max Barber, Richard Wright, and the Harvard-trained Carter G. Woodson.

Carter G. Woodson exemplified the black public intellectual. His tireless efforts at promoting African American history not only went a long way to making that discipline a vital and important part of American history but would be in the forefront of helping the black bourgeoisie make the necessary arguments for the inclusion of black people in the nation's mainstream.[45]

There were other black intellectuals at historically black colleges and universities: most important was W. E. B. Du Bois's return to Atlanta University in the mid-1930s where he produced, among other projects, *Black Reconstruction* after leaving the NAACP over the famous change in direction for black economic improvement. Charles S. Johnson worked at Fisk University and actively became involved in the beleaguered Civil Rights movement in the South.[46]

What was ironic about these intellectuals and their activities was that they were seldom heard by the white populace and only marginally considered by those whites who held powerful political positions and were sympathetic to the needs of blacks. Since the Depression struck the entire nation, any remedies had a trickle-down impact on black Americans. And given segregation in the South and the unwillingness of the Roosevelt administration to do anything to alleviate the miserable conditions of the black poor in the South or the humiliating segregation that all blacks faced daily out of fear of political retaliation from Southern Democrats, it was a wonder that African Americans benefited from the New Deal in any way, shape, or form. That they did accrue some benefits owed more to migration that had happened in the early part of the century, leading to a shift in the ways in which blacks voted, as well as the thinking of many black intellectuals that reforms in the economic arena would aid not only all Americans but African Americans. Here black intellectuals were instrumental, as they were more likely to back the Rooseveltian reforms and view those reforms as a way of not only uplifting the masses of blacks but also as a wedge that would eventually break down segregation and the color barriers to education and jobs.[47]

Once again, in the 1930s the question of class versus race became a resounding theme that would course its way to the present. A key moment in that debate revolved around W. E. B. Du Bois's shift in thinking regarding the economic improvement of African Americans. Du Bois recognized that the New Deal was not helping black people as effectively as it should. He departed from the legalistic and integrationist thrust of the NAACP and announced, "Where separation of mankind into races, groups, and classes is compulsory, either by law or custom, and whether that compulsion is temporary or permanent, the only effective defense that the segregated and despised group has against complete spiritual and physical disaster is internal self-organization for self-respect and self-defense."[48]

This politically inspired stratagem created a heated controversy that has yet to be resolved and has diminished moral capital within black America. Much of the irresolution rests on the fact that for African Americans the quest to maintain a heritage and be accepted into mainstream American society has created a duality that has forced a reconfiguration of American society itself. Thus, Du Bois was not as contradictory as later scholars have come to understand him in this particular stance.[49]

Du Bois departed from the NAACP for over a decade and while his departure to Atlanta University may have cooled the situation down in the NAACP, the social and political implications of what he proposed remained for black intellectuals to grapple with then and now. The question of the efficacy and value of voluntary segregation reemerged in the 1990s as a visibly enlarged black middle class faced an expanding black "underclass," as well as the larger threat of losing those economic gains that they had accrued from the Civil Rights movement and affirmative action. The issues that the black middle class faced were national in scope, as well as particular to African America.

But during the 1930s, this "race versus class" debate took place more within black intellectual circles and political organizations. Outside that circle, the need continued to counter the prevailing racism of the day, whether it came in the form of lynchings or more subtle forms of discrimination as found in covenants that barred blacks from housing or employment opportunities or the immensely humiliating, stifling atmosphere of the Jim Crow South. In this terrain it has to be noted that the federal government was not much help.

It was only after massive reforms that changed the structure of the political economy such that a welfare state was created and World War II opened possibilities nationally and internationally for the struggles for civil rights that the federal government would aid African Americans. As Kenneth O'Reilly has cogently pointed out, the federal government has never done anything for black Americans until they were forced to. Despite the momentous changes in American political culture due to Roosevelt's reforms, he lacked "an appreciation of or sympathy for problems of race and racism in American life."[50]

Thus when the first March on Washington was proposed to demand an end to discrimination in the hiring of workers for the war effort, A. Philip Randolph moved to keep his movement an all-black one to keep it from being dismissed as a ploy of the Left. This brought the conundrum of the strategy of voluntary segregation, which Du Bois had proposed years before, and was organized by class outside the circles of black intellectuals and black organizations. The irony of the situation has not been unnoted; as Kenneth O'Reilly stated, "The greatest antidiscrimination event in the twentieth century's first half began by adopting discrimination as its own policy" (130).

While that situation would not develop in the next March on Washington, in 1963, it was certainly bubbling beneath the surface of an apparently successful integrated effort to heal the nation's racial sores and demand jobs. It is instructive to note that this apotheosis of the movement occurred when Du Bois, who had left America in despair of its ever eradicating racism, died in his newly adopted home of Ghana, a leading standard bearer of African liberation and beacon for many African American intellectuals and activists in Africa. The duality with which he so poignantly described the situation of black Americans and the political stratagem of voluntary segregation, however, continued to haunt, and ultimately debilitate, a movement that was aimed at securing inclusion in American society.

Both the tensions surrounding the "two-ness" of African Americans and the idea of separatism resurfaced in the more youthful and increasingly radical organization the Student Nonviolent Coordinating Committee. This organization began as the embodiment of Martin Luther King Jr.'s vision of the beloved community only to find itself wrestling with the same issue that Du Bois and Randolph faced in the 1930s and '40s: Should blacks exert pressure without whites? Is it always necessary for African Americans to form their own self-governing organizations for the purpose of self-respect? In many respects that was what the Black Power movement was about. It was also about a crack in the foundations of the moral capital that had been set over the many years that black people existed in this country.

Caught up in the changes that were going on in the nation and the world, the young people of SNCC moved from a vision of racial harmony based on respect for the individual to a passionate belief in and defense of liberation for the oppressed of the world. Obsessed with the fact of power and domination, SNCC enacted a variation of Du Bois's voluntary segregation when they dismissed whites from the organization and proclaimed that blacks within SNCC must be allowed to determine their liberation. There was not quite a disbelief in the utility of coalitions, but for that moment separatism was considered the best way to go.[51]

While the Black Power movement served to push many white liberals and radicals to consider that separation might be a worthy enterprise, it did little to resolve the massive problems that faced the black poor and the structural conditions that enlarged the black middle class, who, over a period of time, developed an angst over their role in the United States. African American intellectuals like Bayard Rustin on the left and Thomas Sowell on the right who criticized the Black Power movement were dismissed by the angry militants, who favored the intellectual lights of Malcolm X, Stokely Carmichael, Eldridge Cleaver, Franz Fanon, or other Third World writers.[52]

By the 1980s, the nation had gone through a serious enough backlash against the progress won by the Civil Rights movement that, with the ascension of Ronald Reagan to the presidency, the Civil Rights establishment found itself on the defense. Despite the steady calls for an end to affirmative action, drives toward eliminating welfare measures that assisted the poor, and the resurfacing of a neoscientific racism that claimed the behavior of blacks stemmed from bad genes, there also emerged a new cadre of black intellectuals who attempted not only to combat the increasingly rightward tilt of the nation but to outline a new vision for the twenty-first century. But this group was significantly different from the black intellectuals of the 1930s.

First and foremost, these new black intellectuals were almost always to be found in predominately white institutions of higher learning. These opportunities were the result of civil rights acts and affirmative action from the Johnson administration's Great Society programs. Secondly, this group of intellectuals included highly visible women, who with some influence from the women's movement, added a new perspective to black intellectual discourse. Finally, there developed within this group several strands of thought ranging from black feminism to Afrocentrism and a renewed interest in religion. To be sure, many of these developments reflected ongoing changes that had occurred in the society, especially as the nation moved away from the more progressive ideas of the 1960s and '70s. But the growth of a black intelligentsia was also the result of the enlargement of an educated black middle class who benefited from the Civil Rights movement. This group seemed poised to offer much good not only for African America but also for the nation. But herein lay the dilemma.

For despite the pluses that came from having a large number of black intellectuals, there were minuses that severely hampered their ability to be effective in prescribing or influencing social policies in the nation. Take the matter of the location of the new black intellectuals. While it might have been a positive result to integrate these intellectuals into the academy, the downside was that they had been cut off from the masses of African Americans who were in serious need of their presence. In much the same way as the black middle class has removed itself from the inner cities of the nation to the suburbs and thereby removed role models for the poor, African American intellectuals have little or no connection with those ordinary black folks who may benefit from their thinking.

But probably more important was the fact that there was a serious vacuum regarding black leadership in African America, and the present generation of black intellectuals had not been successful in filling the gap. Why this was had more to do with the inability of the African American intellectuals to resolve the identity crisis or the matter of duality in a society where race and racism are deeply embedded. There was also the continued marginality of black intellectuals in a society that, in the end, continued to be predominately white. This is not to say that black intellectuals have not grappled with this concern; they have done so on all levels from fiction to autobiography to philosophy to critical thinking.[53]

But a highly instructive case of how black intellectuals have been grappling with the duality that Du Bois has spoken of and the vacuum in black leadership was a work of reflective essays, a "revaluation" of Du Bois's notion of the talented tenth and the dual consciousness of that particular group. Presented by two of the late twentieth century's preeminent black intellectuals, Henry Louis Gates Jr. and Cornel West, *The Future of the Race* sounds as if it has all the makings of a manifesto for the neo–black renaissance of the 1990s.[54]

But this slim volume was more about the plight of African America, the black middle class, and the problems inherent in Du Bois's formulation of the talented tenth and, implicitly, double consciousness. The book appeared at a moment when the nation was witnessing a polarization of the races over the issue of affirmative action and the rise of a housing and educational neosegregation by some in the black middle class that had received the tacit approval of liberals and conservatives alike. Indeed, in the centennial anniversary of the infamous *Plessy v. Ferguson* decision, American race relations appeared to be reverting to the notion that there could be a more stable society where blacks and whites were "separate but equal."

Thus Gates and West, echoing Charles Dickens, stated, *"These are the best of times for the black middle class—the heirs of Du Bois's Talented Tenth—it is the worst of times for an equally large segment of our community."*[55] The authors' intention was to critique the 1903 essay by Du Bois, "The Talented Tenth" as well as his revised testament "The Talented Tenth Memorial Address" delivered in 1948; both essays were reprinted in their volume as appendices. But as will be demonstrated, they unwittingly fell into many of the same traps that their predecessors in the 1930s and the 1960s fell into when discussing the entwined nature of race and class. Moreover, their book provided a subtle but revealing portrait of the loss of moral capital that plagued black intellectuals in the waning years of the twentieth century: "We have decided to begin to address these complex issues by rereading the essay that sought to define the 'ethical content' of our 'ethnic identities' as Cornel West has put it—the moral responsibilities of black leadership." (xii)

With this goal in mind, the authors plunged into one of the most crucial issues that have faced black intellectuals: race and class. They proclaimed, "Race differences and class differentials have been ground together in this country in a crucible of misery and squalor, in such a way that few of us know where one stops and the other begins. But we do know that the causes of poverty within the black community are both *structural* and *behavioral*, as the sociological studies of William Julius Wilson have amply demonstrated, and we would be foolish to deny this."

On the surface this statement would go without saying, but a critical reflection reveals that it leaves more out than is warranted. For example, why rely on just William Julius Wilson's studies? There is a rich sociological tradition that demonstrates that their assertion is a hotly contested one. After all, the pioneering study of the urban black community was by the very man whom they are seeking to reevaluate: W. E. B. Du Bois's *The Philadelphia Negro*. And if one reads Kevin Gaines's magisterial study, *Uplifting the Race: Black Leadership, Politics, and Culture in the Twentieth Century,* we find that West and Gates have skimmed over a large body of work that could have strengthened their claim as well as relieved them from the unnecessarily negative baggage that uplift ideology contains. Their assertion seemed even more egregiously unfair when they did not mention black sociologists such as E. Franklin Frazier, Charles S. Johnson, Oliver C. Cox, Elijah Anderson, and Joyce Ladner, to name but a few. There are also white sociologists who have contributed much to the tradition: John Dollard and the man who deeply influenced many black sociologists in the 1930s, Robert Ezra Park.[56]

West and Gates revealed more dramatically the collapse of moral capital when they dealt with the thorny issue of how the black middle class (seemingly synonymous here with the "talented tenth") should politically resume leadership of African America. They state, "We must stand boldly against any manifestation of anti-black racism, whatever form it might take. On this matter, there can be no compromise. But to continue to repeat the same old formulas, to blame 'the man' for oppressing us all, in exactly the same ways; to scapegoat Koreans, Jews, women, or even black immigrants for the failure of African Americans to seize local entrepreneurial opportunities, is to neglect our duty as leaders of our own community" (xv). While this is nicely put, it was also mischievously evasive. By coming out forcefully against "anti-black racism" and then adding a caveat against the scapegoating of Jews, women, and Koreans, among others, West and Gates skirted the issue of black racism. This is clearly a compromised position. They contradict themselves and fail as moral leaders of their community.

The context for this compromise and moral failure rested in their belief that there could be an "operational unity" among black leaders who had divergent ideologies. In other words, there had come to be a belief, in the mid-1990s, that black nationalists and integrationists could form coalitions that would work for the common good of the black community. However, what was lacking in this coalition building was the moral fortitude to erase or at least distance oneself from the most harmful aspects of particular ideologies. This would mean the rigid patriarchalism embedded within the ideology of racial uplift as well as the anti-Semitism and racial chauvinism of some forms of black nationalism.

West and Gates offer several solutions that seemed to reflect the racial uplift ideology of the earlier years of this century. For example, they call for black sophomores and juniors in college to do summer internships in the poorer sections of the black community. They made the usual calls for the government to provide a comprehensive jobs bill. Gates in his reflective essay summed up the matter by stating, "For black America needs a politics whose first mission isn't a reinforcement of the idea of black America; and a discourse of race that isn't centrally concerned with preserving the idea of race and racial unanimity. We need something we don't yet have: a way of speaking about black poverty that doesn't falsify the reality of black advancement; a way of talking about black achievement that doesn't distort the enduring realities of black poverty" (38).

This passage clearly showed an anguished Du Boisian double consciousness. Gates was calling for a multiculturalism that somehow could preserve racial ethnicity. He wanted "race" taken out of the discourse on national problems but not the cultural achievements of African Americans. It was really not at all that clear that this could happen as long as black Americans existed in a society where white Americans denied or were unwilling to look at the social construction of their whiteness. Gates was far too optimistic on the issue of the deep-seated conservatism of the black masses as well.

Neither Gates nor West gave much attention to the reemergence of black conservatism within the black community over the last decade or so. Gates did remark, "Pollsters have long known of the remarkable gap between the leaders and the led in black America. . . . Indeed, on many key issues blacks are more conservative than whites. If the numbers of black Republicans are on the rise, as these opinion surveys suggest, it would be unwise to dismiss the phenomenon" (33).

But it has been axiomatic that blacks are more conservative than their leadership regardless of party affiliation. Benjamin Quarles, the esteemed black historian, pointed out the conservative nature of African Americans many years ago. Even more problematic was Gates's placement of that conservatism historically.[57] For Gates to state that accommodationism turns into separatism and that Minister Louis Farrakhan of the Nation of Islam and Booker T. Washington are "cousins with respect to content" was far too simplistic. The problem here was that Gates's use of "accommodationism" to mean conservatism/ separatism and "integrationism" to mean liberalism/assimilation was far too facile (34). Du Bois, for example, was certainly a proponent of integration but not necessarily of assimilation. Recall that in 1934 he stated that it would be good for blacks to separate and build their own economy. Then they would be able to deal with the dominant majority on an equal basis. It must be remembered that Booker T. Washington also believed in integration; although it was more of a gradual, evolutionary kind.

Henry Louis Gates's contribution to *The Future of the Race,* autobiographical as well as reflective on the concerns of the talented tenth and their need to resume moral leadership, nonetheless contained too many assertions that were tossed off far too breezily. There was an optimism here that bordered on the Pollyannish. But that being the case, Gates's essay stood in stark contrast to Cornel West's philosophic ruminations and critique of Du Bois and the talented tenth. After stating that "Du Bois is the brook of fire through which we all must pass in order to gain access to the intellectual and political weaponry needed to sustain the radical democratic tradition in our time" (55), West launched into a withering critique of Du Bois that indicated West's belief that Du Bois was not black enough to understand the plight of the masses. Du Bois, according to West, "was first and foremost a black New England Victorian seduced by the Enlightenment ethos and enchanted with the American Dream." Du Bois's "inability to immerse himself in everyday life precluded his access to the distinctive black tragicomic sense and black encounter with the absurd" (55).

Although West does cite the magisterial biography of Du Bois by David Levering Lewis (volume 1 was completed at the time and was more relevant for West's purposes), one wonders if he has really *read* Lewis. And while West has certainly read Du Bois, there was an agenda at work that pitted West's fervent belief in radical democracy and cultural nationalism against Du Bois's more universalist humanism. West chided Du Bois for not mentioning or analyzing Ida B. Wells's organizing of the black women's club movement. Even more harshly West stated that Du Bois "never fully understood or appreciated the strong—though not central—Black Nationalist strain in the Black Freedom Movement" (67–68, 72). Like Gates, West was here treading some shaky historical ground.

To begin with his remarks regarding Du Bois and Wells: Ida B. Wells, though certainly an organizer of the club movement, was also fully involved in the antilynching crusade. Du Bois did acknowledge her role in the antilynching movement and wrote about it himself. As for the African American women's club movement, which was organized by upper- and middle-class black women such as Mary Church Terrell, Josephine St. Pierre Ruffin, Fannie Barrier Williams, and Wells, among others: this movement was organized before the rise of Booker T. Washington and Du Bois. One can certainly criticize Du Bois for not giving more attention to that movement. But it should be kept in mind that Du Bois, as befitting the Victorian patriarch of uplift ideology, did not intrude upon this development. Nor did he demean it.[58]

As for Du Bois's lack of feeling for or understanding of the black nationalist strain of the black freedom movement, West never summoned the historical evidence to show this to be the case. David Levering Lewis clearly delineated Du Bois's understanding and coming to grips with pan-Africanism and black nationalism. While it is true that he did not care for Marcus Garvey's movement, he nonetheless begrudgingly acknowledged it. Moreover, Du Bois was highly active in the Pan-African Congresses, which he helped to shape.[59]

Of course Du Bois brought to the table a progressive, American optimism, but that does not mean that he was unaware of the deep pessimism of black nationalism. He just refused to wallow in it. Cornel West, here, and further on in his essay, "Black Strivings in a Twilight Civilization," pandered to late-twentieth-century black nationalists who seemed to have stepped into the vacuum of leadership that was created by the widening division between the black middle class and the urban black poor.

West may have also been reacting defensively given his own compromising actions. His support of Louis Farrakhan's Million Man March of 1996 and Benjamin Chavis's National African American Leadership Summit marked a serious capitulation to moral insensitivity and a diminishment of moral capital given Farrakhan's anti-Semitism and black supremacist views and Chavis's and Farrakhan's sexism. Nonetheless, West noted that "black nationalism is a complex tradition of thought and action, a tradition best expressed in the numerous insightful texts of black public intellectuals like Maulana Karenga, Imamu Amir Baraka, Haki R. Madhubuti, Marimba Ani, and Molefi Asante" (73).

West pointed out that the black nationalist tradition posed a pessimism that ultimately leads to "a state of paralyzing despair." While this is undoubtedly true, one wonders why he took Du Bois to task for being an optimist. West missed a crucial aspect of double consciousness here; that being the ability to measure oneself in a way other than, to use Du Bois's words, "by the tape of a world that looks on in amused contempt and pity." Finally, in his cataloguing of recent black nationalist intellectuals, West negates the truly rich tradition of classical black nationalism as evoked by Alexander Crummell, Edward Wilmot Blyden, Martin Delaney, and Henry Highland Garnet, among many others. But that would have undermined much of what West wants to criticize Du Bois for, as those earlier nationalists also embraced civilizationism and Enlightenment thought.[60]

But Cornel West's greatest faux pas was when he stated, "In our era, scholarship is often divorced from public engagement, and shoddy journalism often settles for the sensational and superficial aspects of prevailing crises" (70). West presented this assessment after heralding the fact that Victorian social criticism "contains indispensable" elements "to future critical thought about freedom and democracy in the twenty-first century." He then listed the towering public intellectuals of the Victorian era and the twentieth century, and they all turned out to be European white men! What was the meaning of this? Where were the towering black intellectuals of these periods: Alexander Crummell, Pauline Hopkins, William H. Ferris, Alice Dunbar-Nelson, William Monroe Trotter, Anna Julia Cooper, Paul Laurence Dunbar, E. Franklin Frazier, Ida Wells-Barnett, Richard Wright, Margaret Alexander Walker, Ralph Ellison, Zora Neale Hurston, James Baldwin, Lorraine Hansberry, Harold Cruse, Toni Morrison, and, of course, W. E. B. Du Bois? And this is only a partial list that could be constructed. Cornel West, in the venerable words of the streets, was shucking and jiving here.

There were some good points that West presented in his essay. In the following passage, there was the promise of a fresh and positive analysis that might have introduced a needed convergence of the histories of African Americans and other ethnic group histories: "If there are any historical parallels between black Americans at the end of the twentieth century and other peoples in earlier times, two candidates loom large: Tolstoy's Russia and Kafka's Prague—soul starved Russians a generation after the emancipation of the serfs in 1861 and anxiety-ridden Central European Jews a generation before the Holocaust in the 1940s" (75).

What followed was arguably the best section in the essay. Yet it lost any connection to the central concern of the piece: Du Bois and the talented tenth. West was disappointed that Du Bois never engaged the intellectuals of these two groups, as they had many insights that could have been used to understand the plight of African Americans. While West may certainly have a point, within the context of history we must understand what Du Bois was doing at the time that West felt he should have been engaging these intellectuals.

First and foremost, Du Bois made a conscious decision, after the Atlanta riot of 1906, to devote himself to the work of seeing black people attain their rights. He did this by involving himself in the editorship and production of the *Crisis*, the magazine of the NAACP. He turned that journal into one of the most effective activist organs for the explanation and justification of black civil rights of that period. When Du Bois left the NAACP and returned to the classroom at Atlanta University, he again took up empirical studies of the black condition in the United States with an eye toward affecting public policy for the alleviation of black poverty. The result of this was the creation of another influential journal, *Phylon*.

Du Bois also devoted himself to understanding the workings of colonialism in Africa and Asia. His tireless work in fighting for the end of colonialism was reflected in the books and essays that he wrote over a long and fruitful period. It is one thing to be disappointed in an intellectual who has not done the work he or she has set out to do, but to be disappointed in a thinker who happens not to read every other thinker whose situation might be analogous is unfair. Du Bois chose the path that he felt was best for the freedom of his people. In so doing he left black intellectuals with much to ponder if not build upon.

Like Henry Louis Gates, Cornel West posited in his essay a solution for the plight of African Americans in the coming century. West called for a radical democracy that would begin where Du Bois ended: "militant despair." This militant despair was the result of Du Bois's struggle for civil rights and equality in this country. It was a despair that led Du Bois to turn his back on America and embrace Africa (Ghana) as his home.

For many, such a starting point would be a shaky proposition, especially since both West and Gates relied heavily on the cultural realm to provide insights into "the tragicomic and absurd character of black life in America." While West recognized the necessity of political engagement, his espousal of a democratic socialism was reduced, given the collapse of concrete socialism in the world, to talking about a "radical democracy" that apparently accepts capitalism but opts for a neoprogressive liberalism. This surely cannot be the best that our present black intellectuals have to offer.

The black middle class and the intellectuals within that class—as heirs of the talented tenth of Du Bois's description—faced a monumental challenge in the coming century. They needed to look within and retrieve/revive the moral capital necessary to begin anew an uplift ideology that was not condescending or contemptuous of the black masses but that was nonetheless firm in its demand that black people take responsibility for their individual and collective actions. In 2008, with the election of Barack Obama as president, that seemed to be the direction that Obama's thought and actions were leading toward.

West's conclusion meant that racism, sexism, and homophobia must be continually fought through education, and where necessary through legal means. There was no doubt that there was a strong conservatism within the black church that vitiated against this important project of tolerance. Yet there was also that essence of moral capital within African America that has always been willing to accept those for who they are as long as the community is not threatened. Likewise the issues surrounding gender must have particular attention paid to them. For far too long, the macho posturing of black males has been tolerated to a degree that is damaging to the community as a whole. It is to their credit that African American women intellectuals have persistently and firmly pointed out that male supremacy has no real place in a community that has been as oppressed as black Americans have been. It was now time for African American men to work with black women in an effort to become aware of the traps that rigid adherence to gender roles can cause within families as well as within the larger community.

And here it was most important that the black middle class and black intellectuals construct a language and vision of integrative cultural diversity that recognized that racial separatism, however attractive it may seem at times, is nonetheless anathema; that it only feeds timeworn notions of racism. In constructing a language around integrative cultural diversity, the African American intelligentsia cannot compromise on the issue of anti-Semitism; that time for healing is long overdue and black intellectuals have yet to clean house on this score.

This also holds true regarding scapegoating of new immigrants of color who are arriving in this country. Resuscitating moral capital means that African American intellectuals and the black middle class must resume the higher ground of tolerance, good faith, belief in the principles of the American creed, and a renewed struggle against the ideologies of racism and xenophobia.

Finally, the black middle class and African American intellectuals must be bold in presenting a new vision of the political economy. This will have to proceed on ideological grounds, both individually and collectively. And it will involve, by necessity, coalitions that are perforce antiracist, antisexist, and in some cases bringing together those who adhere to labels such as radical, liberal, and conservative.

Henry Louis Gates Jr. and Cornel West did not really address any of these matters in depth. As preeminent intellectuals, they should have made the attempt. But there was the queasy sense that what they implicitly concluded was that the so-called crossover generation of modern black intellectuals may be tapped out on these matters.[61]

That implicit conclusion was not particularly persuasive. Culturally, African Americans have only begun to make their presence felt in a positive manner; politically there can and will have to be a force to be reckoned with once black intellectuals get over the fear that Martin Kilson has described as the "anxiety about public life."[62] And that will come about when there is a recognition, respect, and coherence of vision among black and white intellectuals.

3

THE
CONSERVATIVE
REVOLUTION AND
ITS IMPACT ON
AFRICAN AMERICA,
1980–1992

In 1977, George Samuel Schuyler, the "godfather" of black conservatives, passed away and thus went one of the more remarkably enigmatic figures in African American letters. The handsome, dark-skinned Schuyler was born in Providence, Rhode Island, and raised in Syracuse, New York. Upon dropping out of high school, he went into the Army for seven years, saw service in France during World War I, and attained the rank of first lieutenant.

Schuyler then came back to the States and, after some involvement in the labor movement, employment at menial jobs, and habitation with hobos in New York City's Bowery, became a writer for A. Philip Randolph and Chandler Owen's black socialist magazine *The Messenger*. Shortly afterwards he had his own column, "Shafts and Darts: A Page of Calumny and Satire," and began his career as one of African America's counterparts to the social commentator and satirist H. L. Mencken. Schuyler soon became managing editor of the magazine and produced issues that were so incendiary in their tone that Southern members of the House of Representatives moved to investigate it.[1]

George S. Schuyler was a man of many contradictions, especially in regard to race. Politically he went from being a traveler in socialist and union circles and an advocate in creating economic cooperatives to being an ardent ultraconservative. It was his obsession with race that brought out the starkest contradictions. As Henry Louis Gates Jr. wrote in an appreciative essay in the mid-1990s, Schuyler struggled with the Du Boisian dualism of the "two-ness" of the African American. It was a struggle, states Gates, that "is among the most fascinating episodes in American letters." Schuyler was indeed a fascinating man who led a complicated and prolific writing life. He created novels and serialized stories about "Black Internationales" that, as Gates put it, would be an "Afrocentrist's dream."[2]

Yet his first book was titled *Racial Intermarriage in the United States* (1929), and he was a fervent believer in "hybrid vigor": the idea that the children of interracial marriages would be genetically superior and would go on to end racial problems in the nation. In many ways, it was an extreme form of amalgamation and not unlike that which was called for by Frederick Douglass in the late nineteenth century. Schuyler did not just write about this but lived it. He married a white artist from Texas, Josephine Cogdell, and had a daughter, Phillipa Duke Schuyler. They read to her as an infant, and when she was five years old she submitted a composition to the New York Philharmonic. Phillipa would go on to be a musician, composer, and journalist (like her father).[3] Schuyler was very close to his family and particularly proud of his daughter's accomplishments. Whether her genius was the product of "hybrid vigor" or the result of studious and loving parenting, Schuyler was convinced that this was the way to the resolution of racial tensions and problems in the United States. Politically as with his written work, Schuyler was also complex.[4]

It would be fairly easy to read the later George S. Schuyler, who wrote for William Loeb's far-right newspaper, the *Manchester Guardian*, as well as an ongoing column for the John Birch Society, and dismiss him as a crank or a self-hating Negro. But in looking at the various journeys that Schuyler went through politically, racially, and literarily, a different assessment could be made. That assessment would certainly be more complicated, but it would show some consistency to a man who fervently was against the color bar even as he was obsessed by it.

For many of his early years, Schuyler traveled in leftist circles and, as has been noted, wrote for the black socialist magazine *The Messenger*. He knew almost all of the leading lights of the Harlem Renaissance and was well versed in the political and literary controversies of the time. Indeed he was often in the thick of them with pronouncements such as the essay that he wrote for the *Nation* titled "The Negro Art Hokum." In this piece, he went against those who believed that there was a black renaissance in literature and the arts and suggested that there was no such thing. Looking back on the matter, Schuyler said, "Such artistic performance by colored American artists would in the very nature of things be indistinguishable from other American art; that the American Negro was just a lamp blacked Anglo-Saxon, and could no more escape the imprint of his environment than colored people in other lands had done."[5]

Schuyler believed that African Americans were first and foremost Americans. They were discriminated against, and he believed that was wrong (he detested the Jim Crow system in the South, seeing it as a modern form of slavery). But he also believed that African Americans had accomplished much and could do much more if they seized the opportunities around them. In his autobiography, which was written in the 1960s, Schuyler contended, "My feeling was then, and it is stronger now, that Negroes have the best chance here in the United States if they will avail themselves of the numerous opportunities they have. To be sure it is not easy being a black man in the United States but it is easier than anywhere else I know for him to get the best schooling, the best living conditions, the best economic advantages, the best security, the greatest mobility, and the best health."[6]

Harkening back to Frederick Douglass and Booker T. Washington, Schuyler believed that ordinary African Americans needed "more optimism and less pessimism." Schuyler's beliefs would surely have fit well with the conservative tenor of the 1980s and 1990s. Indeed, his statements may have put him into a more moderate camp given that what made Schuyler's views so extreme were his rabid anticommunism and his ferocious dismissal of the Civil Rights movement and the protests that accompanied them. He certainly was not in favor of the Black Power movement. He lamented the praise given to Malcolm X, stating in 1973, "It is hard to imagine the ultimate fate of a society in which a pixilated criminal like Malcolm X is almost universally praised, and has hospitals, schools, and highways named in his memory! . . . We might as well call out the schoolchildren to celebrate the birthday of Benedict Arnold."[7]

But this was not inconsistent with his former beliefs. Schuyler did not think much of Marcus Garvey and the Back to Africa movement in the 1920s. He likened Garvey to Adolf Hitler and said that in many ways Garvey anticipated the rise of Hitler. What most put Schuyler off was the fact that Garvey held a hatred for whites and declared everything black supreme. Here again, the main concern for Schuyler was the notion of color. In his autobiography, he ran down the list of almost every black organization that sought the attention of the masses or was concerned with changing the conditions of black people and in each case he noted that there was hardly a pure Negro in the group (*Black and Conservative*, 122–24).

The color line infuriated Schuyler, yet he was loath to really mount an offensive against it. As much as he believed that black people should be accorded the rights that all Americans had, he nonetheless believed, "Once we accept the fact that there is, and always will be, a color caste system in the United States, and stop crying about it, we can concentrate on how best to survive and prosper within that system. This is not defeatism but realism. It is tragic and pointless to wage war against the more numerous and more powerful white majority, and to jeopardize what advantages we possess" (*Black and Conservative*, 121–22).

If Schuyler's remarks seem more than confusing, it has to be noted that above all he prided individualism and character building. He did not see African Americans as inferior, nor can it be argued that he hated black people. Schuyler actually believed that black people would be better off just going about their business of being good, God-fearing, hard-working individuals who used their talents to survive and prosper. Race should just be ignored.

Of course, Schuyler did believe that there was a black folk tradition that he situated in the South. As he said, "When the Negroes talked about the 'Old Country,' they meant Virginia, the Carolinas, and the Deep South." And he was quite astute as to the fact that there was more intermixture among the black population of the United States than in the rest of the Western Hemisphere. He recognized that there were very few pure black people in the United States; that the mixture of whites, Indians, and Africans had created a multicolored group and that the reigning "one-drop rule" (which declared anyone with one drop of Negro blood to be black) prohibited the color caste system that was prevalent in the Caribbean and Latin America. In many ways, Schuyler saw the problems for the black masses coming more from their socioeconomic status than from their color (*Black and Conservative*, 119).

How then to explain the wonderfully fantastic serial that he produced under the pseudonym Samuel I. Brooks for the *Pittsburgh Courier*: "The Black Internationale" and "Black Empire"? Were they really the creation of a man who had fragmented himself as Henry Louis Gates suggested in an early 1990s appraisal of Schuyler and his work? Or can there be seen a consistency, a need to demonstrate that black people are human beings capable of making empires and conquering lands and being fascists?[8]

The career of George Schuyler was rich and deep enough to create a complex work of "black utopian fantasies." And there may be some truth to the argument that he was much like the black man that Du

Bois spoke of, with his two-ness ever warring and struggling to find a truer and better self. But it could also be argued that Schuyler was charting a path for future black conservatives to elaborate upon. His contemporary in the 1920s and '30s, Zora Neale Hurston, certainly was on a similar path.[9]

Both Hurston and Schuyler were deeply embedded in a grand American tradition: that of reinventing oneself. Both recognized the integral role that black people played in the American experience, but unlike Ralph Ellison, who would celebrate and adumbrate that black experience within the American experience, Hurston and Schuyler saw the black experience as secondary or at most exotic and rustic. Hurston used her training as an anthropologist under the tutelage of Franz Boas to study and preserve Southern rural black folk culture. Given that she was born in the Deep South and was raised in an all-black town, Hurston saw black folk culture as part of an American way of life that most Americans were not exposed to. For Hurston, the experience of growing up in an all-black environment away from the harsher realities of segregation enabled her to see black people living and working as individuals and not just as a victimized racial group.[10] Thus her bitter satire of those "Niggerati" in the Harlem Renaissance reflected her belief that race consciousness was too one-sided. As she expressed in her essay "How It Feels to Be Colored Me," "I do not belong to the sobbing school of Negrohood who hold that nature some how has given them a low down dirty deal and whose feelings are all hurt about it. Even in the helter-skelter skirmish that is my life, I have seen that the world is to the strong regardless of a little pigmentation more or less. No, I do not weep at the world—I am too busy sharpening my oyster knife."[11]

Hurston's studious attention to preserving the Southern rural black culture was played out in her social scientific studies and her fiction. At her very best she was way ahead of many in the Harlem Renaissance in looking at issues of gender relations. At worst she might be accused of turning a blind eye to the harsh realities of the black experience in America.

Hurston died penniless in a welfare home in Florida in January 1960. Her work influenced much of the writing that would be undertaken in the late 1970s and the 1980s by African American women who were a part of the Civil Rights movement generation. But it would not be until the 1980s when Alice Walker would rescue Hurston from the obscurity that befell her in the '50s. What was left out of the rescue was her political views.[12] In a decade when the Reagan revolution had put the left-leaning African American literary establishment and black leadership on the defensive, Hurston's conservative views were hardly mentioned. The fact that she, like Schuyler, was critical of the Supreme Court's *Brown v. Board of Education* decision and that she was not opposed to segregation as such put her at odds with most African Americans who were in the forefront of fighting for black rights.[13]

As a critic of demonstrations and what would later come to be called the "Civil Rights establishment," George Schuyler and Zora Neale Hurston may have spoken the thoughts of many ordinary African Americans who did not see themselves as victims on the one hand and on the other just wanted to be left alone albeit with the rights that all whites had. Schuyler was convinced that it would only take "Negro ingenuity" to quietly solve the discriminations in housing and other areas. Hurston, in her autobiography, *Dust Tracks on the Road*, saw demonstrations against discrimination and cries for integration as potentially harmful for black-owned businesses that did invaluable service in the black community.[14]

Schuyler railed against the black leadership from Martin Luther King Jr. to Malcolm X, seeing them as being manipulated by the communists. While Schuyler granted that black organizations had done much to ameliorate the conditions of African Americans, he remained firm in his belief that "after all, the welfare of Negroes is primarily the responsibility of Negroes" (*Black and Conservative*, 122). This belief in communal self-help is a hallmark tradition in African America and is the touchstone of black conservatism.

If it were not for Schuyler's obsession with the notion of a communist conspiracy out to take over not only the Civil Rights movement but also all of America, he may have been taken more seriously by black leaders in the more traditional civil rights organizations such as the NAACP and the National Urban League. But there were other conservative voices in African America that would come to the fore and take up where Schuyler stopped.

By the time that George Schuyler's autobiography saw its second printing in 1971, a young economist, Thomas Sowell, was moving toward inheriting the mantle of black conservatism. Born in South Carolina and educated at Harvard and the University of Chicago, Sowell studied the economic theories of Karl Marx and for a time considered himself a Marxist/leftist. But that soon changed, ironically, as the Civil Rights revolution was commencing. While Sowell was certainly against discrimination and felt that laws securing the rights of blacks were good, he soon became disillusioned with the social policies of the Great Society programs under Johnson and moved toward what would be later termed a neoconservative position that focused on the need for government restraint in managing human behavior and cultural discipline on the part of African Americans and Americans in general.[15]

This position had some roots in earlier African American thought that emanated from Booker T. Washington. But Sowell, unlike George Schuyler, was not as race conscious and spent much of his academic career producing studies that showed ethnic minorities getting ahead without the need for affirmative action on the part of government. For Sowell, the capitalist market, kept open to all, would provide the opportunities for any individual who took advantage of it to succeed.[16]

Sowell's neoconservatism emerged in the context of the expansion of educational and professional opportunities for African Americans in the 1970s. As more and more black Americans entered colleges (owing to affirmative actions policies of the late 1960s and early '70s) and the government began to shift its resources from discrimination in small business (through policies initiated by President Nixon) to other arenas, the black middle class began to grow. This growth saw a rise in black professionals who were not politically oriented to the militant nationalism of those on the black left.[17]

While the growing black middle class voted in the Democratic column, by the beginning of the 1980s, there was a small cadre of African Americans who considered themselves "dissenters" from the now-established belief that African Americans deserved rights through affirmative action because of past discriminations. This minimalist idea of reparations for previous years of discrimination became the focus of a general critique by the black neoconservatives, who argued, along with white conservatives, that because affirmative action was about reparations and the alleviation of the victimization of black people, it was tantamount to reverse discrimination. Moreover, affirmative action, it was argued, unfairly stigmatized black people because, as a government handout, it was stating that blacks were not as qualified as whites for professional jobs.[18]

The heated debate over affirmative action was a clear signal to black liberals that the political climate was shifting to the right. As the decade of the 1970s saw the celebration of the nation's bicentennial, the economy was stagnant; there was a growing concern about the large unemployment of black youth in the inner cities; and the nation seemed weary of struggles over race. Yet despite the election of Jimmy Carter, a moderate Democrat from Georgia whose political views on race placed him in the liberal column in the South, the nation moved away from ameliorating the conditions that continued to beset African America.

About the best that could be said for the Carter administration is that it showed that the African American middle class was coming into its own. Carter appointed more liberal African Americans to political positions in Washington than his predecessors, numbers that would stand until the next Democratic president, William Jefferson Clinton, in the 1990s.[19]

With the election of Ronald Reagan to the presidency in 1980 there was a decided shift in the way that American politics would react to the concerns of African Americans. Those on the black left saw the Reagan administration as not the dawning of a new day in America but the closing of the door on almost twenty years of government activity on behalf of civil rights for African Americans. Reagan's belief in the limited government of conservatism did not disallow government intervention, however. The 1980s marked the emergence of a general attempt by the Right to roll back the excesses of the 1960s, particularly within the social realm. That meant an all-out offensive that in the 1990s would be dubbed the "Culture Wars." The offensive, instigated by those on the right who were of a religious cast but certainly not dominated by them, sought to have government control rock music and sexual behavior and restore family values, nuclear family values. Underlying much of the rhetoric and proposed legislation was a racial subtext. There was deep concern about the quality of life in the inner cities of the nation. One of the unintended but tragic results of the enlargement of the black middle class was the removal of that class from the urban areas to the suburbs. It is perhaps too much to say that this was a result of integration, for many African Americans who went to the suburbs faced resistance from the white inhabitants who often left, thus creating black suburbs. Then too, real estate agencies and banks engaged in what was known as "redlining": targeting certain areas of housing as off limits to black people whether or not they could afford the property.[20]

But for those left behind in the slums of America, life became a veritable hell. Schools were inadequate and often arenas of crime. The streets were more than mean; they could be deadly, as the rise of open drug usage led to gang fighting over turf that harmed many an innocent bystander not only on the street but even within homes. The rise in crime went hand in hand with the high rate of unemployment. In the early 1980s, over 40 percent of African American youths were unemployed and without the skills for employment in a rapidly evolving technological society.[21]

Having nothing to do and given the absence of the role models for success that the black middle class could, and once did, provide, young black males often fell into a vicious cycle of crime and irresponsible sexual behavior. The rise in the illegitimate birth rate in the 1980s alarmed just about everyone, yet the solutions fell along predictable lines. Liberals excoriated the callousness and mean-spiritedness of the conservative Reagan administration and called for the creation of more jobs and educational opportunities. Conservatives countered with the call for residents of the inner cities to rehabilitate themselves by changing their behavior. The intellectual listened to most by the Reagan administration, economist George Gilder, called on black males to take the responsibility of fatherhood more seriously and enter the job market with a commitment to keeping their families together.[22] Another intellectual favorite of the Reagan group, Charles Murray, called for an overthrow of the welfare system, which he believed was not only stunting black development but also destroying the general social fabric.[23]

Black conservative intellectual economists such as Glenn Loury and Thomas Sowell concurred and further suggested a restoration of the old uplift ideology of the late nineteenth and early twentieth centuries. Such prescriptions certainly had some merit, but they seemed too small a remedy compared to the vast immiseration that faced many inner-city inhabitants. There was also the presumption by black conservatives (and some black liberals) that only the African American community should clean up the social impoverishment of those in the black masses. For some African American intellectuals such as Randall Kennedy, this was the wrong way to go. He declared that this was a national problem which all Americans had to face.[24]

The 1980s, then, were focused on which strategy would best ameliorate the poverty of the inner cities. Those African American intellectuals on the left favored a governmental solution that addressed the structural inequities that impeded opportunities for education and jobs. African American intellectuals on the right (and later in the center) favored what could be called a behavioral approach. They wanted African Americans to lift themselves not only economically but also morally. Here the emphasis was on the individual's having the right motivation for pursuing the good life. That was to be found in stabilizing the family (for example, black males should take responsibility for fathering children) and eschewing violent behavior (here the "Just Say

No" antidrug message of the Reagan administration was supposed to apply). While again these were laudable efforts, they had been tried before with only minor success. For example, the Nation of Islam had long made its reputation in the urban communities of black America as an organization that took the most at-risk and even criminal youth and transformed them into upright, responsible people.[25]

In the mid-1970s after Elijah Muhammad died, there was a splintering of the organization, with many of the members following Wallace Muhammad into orthodox Islam. Louis Farrakhan, a protégé of Malcolm X who later turned away from him, re-created the Nation of Islam in the 1980s. Farrakhan attempted to build upon the growth of the black middle class, who had assets that could be tapped to aid those youth gone astray in the inner city. Thus his focus was on reaching out to those in the middle class and to African American youth on college campuses around the country. It was an interesting strategy, but Farrakhan added a new dimension: entry into the political arena.[26]

The Nation of Islam had refrained from getting involved in American politics because of its belief in the separation of the races and the desire to see black people have a nation of their own. In the 1980s that changed. Much of the reason for Farrakhan's growing interest in leading the Nation of Islam into politics had to do with the perception that the Reagan administration disregarded the interests of the African American community and the attempts by the defeated Democratic Party to win back those white middle-class suburbanites who had abandoned the party for Reagan.[27]

Into this shifting mix of political realignment stepped Jesse Jackson, the apparent heir to Martin Luther King Jr., who during the 1970s had spent much of his time in Chicago founding and operating Operation PUSH (People United to Save Humanity). The goal of PUSH was to advance economic parity for African Americans. It was an organization that was modestly successful and provided Jackson with a base of support for future political activity. Jackson became skilled at getting white corporations and businesses to integrate and introduce diversity into their workplaces. From Coca-Cola to Burger King to Kentucky Fried Chicken to Anheuser-Busch, Jackson won benefits for African Americans in terms of jobs in management and franchises. He was even successful in getting the CBS affiliate in Chicago to hire a black manager after the station replaced a black anchor with a white anchor.[28]

Jackson recognized that careful planning along with the mining of the black middle class and those whites who were allies could make a difference in the political sphere. It was clear to Jackson that Ronald Reagan had won the 1980 election because of a coalition of the wealthy and the unregistered, that is, those wealthy white Republicans who wanted a return to the values of free enterprise and a strong God-fearing America and the vast numbers of unregistered black voters, most of whom were in the South. Speaking on the twentieth anniversary of the March on Washington, Jesse Jackson made it clear what his political intentions were about. "Hands that picked cotton in 1884 will pick the president in 1984."[29]

It was here that the convergence of Jackson and the Nation of Islam began. Jackson needed to have the backing of the black leadership establishment and he also needed a lot of money if he was going to make a run for the presidency. The black leadership still clung to the Democratic Party as the best hope of getting help for the black community. They also feared that if large numbers of Afro-Americans voted for a black candidate, then the Republicans would continue to win presidential and even congressional elections (Franklin and Moss, 540).

Jackson forged ahead, convinced that black voters, who had been making impressive changes at the local level in electing mayors in major cities across the United States, including Harold Washington in Jackson's own city, Chicago, could be marshaled to make changes on the national level. Where Jackson did find support was from those disparate groups on the left who needed something to help them to reform a cohesive movement. Jackson fit the bill when he formed, with their support, the "Rainbow Coalition." This was the political vehicle by which Jackson hoped to run for the presidency and challenge the reigning conservatism of the Reagan Republicans and the indifference of the Democrats (Franklin and Moss, 540).

When Jackson made an off-the-record remark to a *Washington Post* reporter about New York City being "Hymie Town," he created a storm of controversy that reflected the strong tensions still existing between blacks and Jews since the late 1960s. It also overshadowed his bid for the presidency as he was forced to make apologies for his remarks. But by the time he made what amounted to a national apology at the Democratic National Convention in 1984, he had included Louis Farrakhan in his delegation. Farrakhan had made statements of his own about Jews and Judaism that angered many and exacerbated the tensions between African American and Jewish people.[30]

He complained that his remarks were taken out of context, but there could be no mistaking that the remarks "Judaism is a gutter religion" and "Hitler was wickedly smart" had a vicious tone to them. It was unlike a black organization to make implicit, let alone overt, anti-Semitic statements. Traditionally, black leaders from across the ideological spectrum had called on the black masses to emulate Jewish people who valued education, social justice, and responsibility highly. That Farrakhan and later his chief aide Kalid Muhammad would make such virulent statements about Jews or Catholics or even blacks who criticized them revealed an ugly side that Jackson or any serious leader would have wanted to contain.[31]

Yet there was very little criticism of Farrakhan and his minions within black intellectual circles, particularly on the left. When there was, as in the case of Julius Lester's critiques in the *New Republic* in 1985 and Henry Louis Gates Jr. in the *New York Times* in 1992, there were outcries from some black intellectuals that it was unfair of white America or Jews to expect black leaders to publicly denounce Farrakhan when many white leaders had said harmful things about blacks but were not reprimanded. Much of this reaction occurred in a climate when many liberal African Americans felt that their stature and the social policies of the 1960s were under attack by the Reagan administration and the nation's rightward shift.[32]

Nonetheless there appeared to be a moral lapse among some black intellectuals. Black leaders seemed to have forgotten that various Reagan administrators who made racially demeaning comments were exposed by the press and were forced by that exposure to apologize or in some cases resign. A prime example of this was Secretary of the Interior James Watts's remark about a commission that he oversaw. "I have a black, I have a woman, two Jews, and a cripple," he stated. He was forced to resign in October 1983. Despite the turn to conservatism in the 1980s, it was still impolitic to make overtly racist remarks.[33]

Farrakhan's presence in African American political circles would prove to be more troublesome for black intellectuals than for conservative whites. The Nation of Islam's basic ideology, despite the thin veneer of progressive rhetoric, was essentially conservative. The NOI forbade their women from taking strong stances with regard to men and their position as head of the household. Women were to be dutiful wives who never questioned their husbands' activities. In return, men were supposed to treat their wives with respect and grant them the space domestically to raise children properly in the faith. These matters came to light when a book by NOI woman writer Scheherazade Ali became a cause célèbre in the late 1980s and early '90s. In her book, which was an inspirational/how-to guide to treating the black woman, most of the Black Muslim ideology with regard to relationships was presented.[34]

Homosexuality was severely frowned upon; so was interracial dating. Politically, African Americans were to do for themselves, as the federal government could not be trusted to help black people. African Americans were brainwashed by the white man's thinking and culture, and must begin to find their true selves. Scheherazade Ali made the rounds of the talk shows, which were beginning to decline into sensationalism, and exacerbated the controversy that focused on her writing that it was okay for a man to slap a woman if she was getting out of hand. This was of course inflammatory in and of itself, given the increased awareness in America of violence against women. But it completely overshadowed the strong conservative messages that were being imparted by the Nation of Islam.[35]

In many respects, these notions were not that much different from what the Christian Right was advocating, and in many ways conservatives in the government or in the Christian Coalition were willing to overlook Farrakhan's anti-Semitic references. But for African American intellectuals, the Nation of Islam posed a dilemma. Should they be allowed to participate with other black leaders on setting the agenda for African America? What of the anti-Semitic statements and ideology in the Nation's thinking? How were those to be handled? Finally, was there really a large constituency for Farrakhan and what did that imply?[36]

These questions would prove to be difficult ones. They haunt African American intellectuals to the present. But for in the current discussion they are brought up to show that African American politics were, despite any conservative shift, taken seriously by the country. Race, the perennial American dilemma, remained in the forefront of American concerns.

If Farrakhan's presence proved unsettling for black intellectuals, particularly those on the left, the rise of black conservatives from within the enlarged professional black middle class proved how entrenched the victories of the Civil Rights movement had become and how scattered the Left was. Even though in the 1980s those activists attempted to pull together a movement that could carry on the legacies of the 1960s, the '80s and '90s proved to be more about sorting through and revising those legacies rather than building on them. It was here that the black conservatives, or "dissenters" as many called themselves, were a crucial part of the dialogue.

While progressive people were protesting the Reagan administration's foreign policies in El Salvador and Nicaragua, Reagan was mounting a domestic counterrevolution to change the social landscape that had been transformed by the Great Society programs of the 1960s. For the nation's black citizens, this meant subtle and sometimes not so subtle attacks on the successes of the previous twenty years. Two areas that came under concentrated attack were the Voting Rights Act and affirmative action.

The Voting Rights Act was due to be evaluated in the early 1980s. Reagan wanted it removed, feeling that it had done its job and that there was no need for it to continue. Indeed, the act had been successful in getting numerous black citizens elected to offices in their locales. Maynard Jackson and then Andrew Young were African American mayors of Atlanta, and that city would continue to see black mayors elected into the 1990s. Tom Bradley, a former officer with the Los Angeles Police Department, had become that city's first black mayor for close to twenty years. And in the nation's capital, the former president of SNCC, Marion Barry, became the city's first African American mayor.[37] The same scenario was repeated throughout the nation in the statehouse and even in the federal government. The Congressional Black Caucus grew from a handful of sixteen members when it was first created in the 1960s to over twenty in the 1990s.

And yet many African Americans were unregistered to vote. This was what propelled Jesse Jackson into running for the White House. Given that voter turnout had declined greatly since the Watergate debacle and the resignation of Richard Nixon in 1974, there was good reason to believe that a strong showing by African Americans at the polls might keep many of the policies that were set in place during the 1960s from being overturned. The Reagan administration was determined, however, to limit, if not eliminate, what it saw as the "Civil Rights establishment."

Reagan moved to do this early in his tenure. In November 1981, he informed the chairman of the Civil Rights Commission, Arthur Fleming, that he was going to be replaced. This was a radical move, as the commission had, since 1957, been very independent and been a watchdog over the policies set by the president. Until Reagan, presidents did not interfere with this bipartisan group even when they were criticized by it. Now for the first time in twenty-four years, Reagan was replacing the chair. He nominated Clarence Pendleton, an African American businessman who had been executive director of the San Diego chapter of the NAACP and was a friend of Attorney General Edwin Meese III. Reagan then nominated to a seat on the commission a black

Philadelphia evangelical minister, B. Sam Hart. In Hart and Pendleton, Reagan found people whose views were the same as Reagan and his conservative brethren. What distinguished Reagan was his willingness to seek out black conservatives whose views were close to his own on matters such as affirmative action and school busing.[38]

Both Pendleton and Hart were avowed opponents of affirmative action. When Hart removed himself from the list of nominees, Reagan went after the three liberals on the commission who most opposed his views on affirmative action: Mary Frances Berry, Blandina Cardenas Ramirez, and Murray Saltzman. To replace them, Reagan nominated Morris Abrams, John Bunzel, and Robert Destro. This attempt at restructuring the commission embroiled the administration in intense wrangling with the House and the Senate. After compromises were set up and undermined, it was finally concluded that the incumbents (Berry, Ramirez, and Saltzman) could stay while Reagan could retain Pendleton as chair and appoint two additional commissioners, John Bunzel and Morris Abrams.[39] Thus, while the Civil Rights Commission was not destroyed, it was badly weakened. No longer did it engage itself in making reports on cases of discrimination or conducting hearings. Now the commission chair made pronouncements that were congenial to conservatives opposed to affirmative action, school busing, and other issues regarding civil rights.

If the Civil Rights Commission suffered badly during the Reagan years, other areas of the government that had protected African Americans' civil rights came under scrutiny with the same intention of removing them or limiting their authority. In the Department of Justice, the Civil Rights Division, under the leadership of Reagan appointee William Bradford Reynolds, began to change the way government viewed affirmative action cases, school busing, and other forms of discrimination. More often than not they opposed all of these and placed the burden of proof for discrimination on the individuals discriminated against rather than the discriminators.[40]

It was clear that Reagan wanted to roll back the gains of the Civil Rights era, particularly certain provisions in the Civil Rights Act of 1964 and the Voting Rights Act of 1965. Reagan wanted to reduce what he believed was a fifty-year control and expansion of the government by liberals. Civil rights were not about freeing African Americans from the oppression of Jim Crow segregation or racism; they were about unnecessary intervention into the lives of American citizens. It was the imposition of liberal social engineering that left Americans with no freedom of voluntary association and cost too much money (Franklin and Ross, 535–38).

For a society that was in deep economic straits when he arrived in office, Reagan's antigovernment ideas resonated with millions of Americans. With unemployment at 8.5 percent and inflation running at 13 percent, Americans were willing to listen to ideas about cutting taxes and ridding the nation of bureaucratic structures that impeded opportunities. They were also vulnerable to blaming scapegoats for causing those economic woes.[41]

Reagan probably did not consider himself a racist or even prejudiced. On one occasion when campaigning for the presidency, he told a group of black Republicans that he was not a bigot. It could also be pointed out that he appointed African Americans in certain positions that had visibility. But it was more likely that these appointments reflected his ideological beliefs rather than a conscious ploy at playing a political race game.[42]

Nonetheless, once in office he refused to meet with black leaders, he was reluctant to sign the act that made Martin Luther King's birthday a national holiday (after various activists, artists, and scholars worked fifteen years for the commemoration), and he continued to oppose the Civil Rights Act of 1964. In Supreme Court Justice Thurgood Marshall's view, Reagan's presidency was "the worst in the White House since Herbert Hoover."[43]

Reagan saw African American needs as a "special interest" and felt that there was a moral imperative to attaining racial justice, not a governmental one. Yet he and his staff opposed welfare and consistently tried to demonize it to the American public. By speaking in code, the Reagan administration was able to portray welfare as a grand handout to poor black Americans despite the fact that they were disproportionately impoverished given their numbers in the nation. Terms such as "welfare queen" were linked in the public mind with race. David Stockman, the president's budget director, stated bluntly, "I don't think people are entitled to services. . . . I don't accept that equality is a moral principle." Stockman had even flirted with New Left politics when he was in college. But he had seen the light, so to speak, and became the major force in the Reagan administration's assault on welfare and social programs that had been erected in the Johnson years.[44]

Even more interesting was the way in which the Reagan counterrevolution used many of the tactics that the New Left used during the antiwar movement. This could be seen in regard to the anti-abortion movement. Year after year since the 1973 *Roe v. Wade* Supreme Court decision that permitted abortions, foes on the religious right and social conservatives demonstrated in Washington and at birth control clinics where abortions were performed. It was a strange turnabout as the progressive forces that favored abortion were able to use the law to protect their interests. They were on the inside while the Right was fighting a battle for the hearts and minds of Americans on this volatile issue.[45]

In the same way the Reagan administration appropriated portions of Martin Luther King Jr.'s ideas on race relations. Where King had spoken of having a dream where people would be judged by the content of their character rather than the color of their skin, many conservatives took this notion of a "color-blind" society and made it the cornerstone of their policies against not only affirmative action but the civil rights acts as well. Black conservatives in particular took this tack.[46]

In the early 1990s, an English professor at San Jose State University in California used "the content of our character" as the title of his book of essays that developed this theme from an African American perspective. While Shelby Steele was not a conservative in the vein of George Schuyler—he was more of a disillusioned liberal who turned to the right—he nonetheless believed that African Americans had gotten caught up in the race game to their detriment. Believing that the war for rights and opportunities had been won, Steele wanted black Americans to move beyond race and begin to develop themselves as American individuals.[47]

Steele shared a fervent belief in integration with Schuyler, but he was of a generation that had seen the move from civil rights based on individual redress to discrimination to black power based on the demand for rights and opportunities for groups. The emergence of group identity politics that was ushered in by the Black Power movement and institutionalized during the Nixon years pervaded the American political landscape in the Reagan years. It was this identity politics, which was accused of imposing "political correctness" on society and said to be in favor of preferential treatment of women and minorities at the expense of merit and standards, that Steele and Glenn Loury lashed out against.[48]

Loury, a beneficiary of affirmative action, having been rescued from the harsh streets of Chicago's South Side, held that legislation and judicial decisions could not give black Americans those things that could be "won through the outstanding achievements of individual black persons." Both men decried the victimization mode that they felt African Americans relied on in order to gain opportunities. Steele argued that affirmative action "nurtures a victim-focused identity in blacks and sends us the message that there is more power in our past suffering than in our present achievements." Loury argued for a change in the behavior of inner-city youth who were at risk of getting into drugs and crime. Loury believed, as did Steele, that the Civil Rights movement had been successful in opening up opportunities for blacks (as individuals) to make it in society.[49]

The difference between Loury and Steele centered on the strategies by which poor African Americans were to overcome their plight. Steele wanted black Americans to take advantage of the opened-up opportunities and mainstream into American society. Loury was in favor of those who had made it giving back to the community through being role models or investing time with youth at risk. Loury's tack was reminiscent of the uplift ideology of the late nineteenth and early twentieth centuries and owed much to the strategy that Booker T. Washington advocated. Then the emphasis was on vocational training and the inculcation of values such as the work ethic, sobriety, and thrift.[50]

It was not just black conservatives who turned their attention to improving conditions in the black community. As the 1980s moved into the '90s, religious leaders grappled with what Cornel West termed the "nihilism" of black youth in the inner cities of America. Reverend Calvin O. Butts of Abyssinian Baptist in Harlem, Reverend Johnny Youngblood of the South Bronx, and Reverend Eugene Rivers III of the Azusa Pentecostal Church in Roxbury, Boston, moved to rescue young blacks from the nihilism that created a swath of self-destruction through drugs, AIDS, black-on-black violence, and the imprisonment of black males far out of proportion to their numbers in the general populace. After more than a decade of this crushing immiseration, it had become clear that what social scientists and commentators had viewed as a "black underclass" had laid waste to a generation of youth. Where white conservatives, and some black conservatives, decried the behavior of those in the inner cities and laid the blame on the welfare system and the amoral culture of poverty, other black conservatives like Robert Woodson and progressives like Eugene Rivers believed that the work of improvement must come from within the communities.[51]

Woodson wanted to use an entrepreneurial approach: setting up small businesses and training blacks in the ways of the information age and the new technologies. Reverend Rivers approached matters from a spiritual and moral perspective. But he also recognized that there was a systemic problem with the United States. Like Cornel West only without the overtly Marxist perspective, Eugene Rivers saw the impoverishment of African Americans resulting from an America caught up in consumerism, glamorization of violence, and disrespect of women. Worst of all, young blacks were lacking in the skills to even be able to compete for the kinds of jobs that the next century would require.[52]

The search for ways to relieve the immiseration of the black inner-city poor continued throughout the 1990s and oftentimes overlapped ideological lines. But there was no doubt that black conservatives were making their voices heard whether it was through journalists and radio commentators such as Armstrong Williams and Ken Hamblin or PBS producer Tony Brown. These conservative voices sounded much like the voices of past black intellectuals and leaders who called for a moral and economic rehabilitation of the black masses. Back then there was the dual struggle not only calling for uplift but also fighting a pervasive racism that labeled all blacks as inferior. With the successes brought about by the Civil Rights movement and the subsequent growth of the black middle class, however, the struggle now centered on getting the black poor to take advantage of the opportunities that were available.

Even though there was an economic downturn in the early 1908s, by the '90s the economy had picked up considerably and the African American masses were beginning to make headway in the struggle against poverty. By the end of the century, *Newsweek* was announcing on its cover and in the lengthy story within that African American males were profiting well with the economic upturn. But even as things were beginning to show improvement, there was stirring on the political front that showed that the influence of black conservatism promised to be around for a long time to come.[53]

When Supreme Court justice Thurgood Marshall decided to step down from the bench in 1991, the end of an era of judicial activism was clearly apparent. President George H. W. Bush's nomination of Clarence Thomas for the position threw black America into an ambivalence that was only worsened as the Senate Judiciary Committee carried out hearings on Thomas's credentials. Thomas was a Reagan appointee to the Department of Education in 1981. Later he was appointed the head of EEOC and then, under President Bush, was appointed a judgeship on the U.S. Court of Appeal for the District of Columbia. His political ideologies were decidedly conservative.

Thomas came to that conservatism by way of an interest in the ideologies of black nationalism as promulgated during the Black Power movement of the late 1960s and '70s. Born poor in Pin Point, Georgia, Thomas attended Catholic boarding schools and then went on to Holy Cross College in Worcester, Massachusetts. Thomas, like many young blacks of the time, became angry at the treatment that African Americans received and gravitated first toward Malcolm X and then toward the separatist politics of the more militant Black Powerites.[54]

But all that changed as the 1970s progressed. Thomas found himself practicing law after graduating from Yale and developing his ideas concerning natural law and the law of nations. Perhaps it was his strong religious beliefs that pushed him to abandon separatism and accept integration. These religious beliefs certainly had much to do with his anti-abortion stance. And it may be that his impoverished childhood in Georgia coupled with the strong discipline that he received from his grandparents and subsequent schooling made him a strong believer in lifting oneself up. Whatever the circumstances that made Thomas a conservative, he wasted little time in stating his dislike for affirmative action (it unfairly stigmatized blacks), the welfare system (it made African Americans dependent on the government and took away their initiative to work), and black leadership (they had created a "cult mentality" that seduced blacks into politically correct positions).[55]

Furthermore, he believed that in judicial matters there was a higher law (a natural law that emanated from God) that would be obeyed. But during the hearings for his nomination for the Supreme Court, Thomas shied away from these controversial aspects of his ideas. At first it seemed that President Bush's nominee would be cleared without too much difficulty. Even the major civil rights organizations seemed unsure of whether or not to support Thomas. Then a serious threat was raised from a former employee of Thomas. Anita Hill was a law professor who taught at the University of Oklahoma. She was a modest and conservative young woman who went to Washington and worked under Clarence Thomas first at the Department of Education and then at EEOC. She claimed that Thomas sexually harassed her at the EEOC with obscene jokes and lewd references to pornographic movies. While these were certainly serious charges, the Judiciary Committee soon found itself overwhelmed; other matters, such as Thomas's contempt for civil rights policy in the EEOC, were shoved into the background.

What followed was one of the most lurid episodes in modern American history. The nation watched as the Judiciary Committee, made up of fourteen white male senators, questioned dozens of African American men and women who spoke on behalf of Thomas or Hill. There were also white defenders of both parties, but what came through was some of the best and brightest of the newly enlarged black professional class providing statements for Thomas or Hill. Sadly, the display was in the course of the "her word against his" argument between two black professionals. Some black male professionals such as John Doggett, a lawyer from Texas, accused Hill of harboring erotic fantasies about every man that she met. Leading figures in the women's movement moved quickly to use Hill's situation as a prime example of what went on in the nation's workplaces and renewed their efforts to have sexual harassment eradicated.[56]

But it was the ugly stereotypes surrounding sex and race that resurfaced in ways that were disturbing not only to black America but also to the nation as a whole. Thomas vehemently denied the charges, despite the fact that Hill presented a calm, steady, and deeply detailed testimony. The most stinging twist to the whole debacle was Thomas's retreat into a strategy that he had spent much of his career excoriating other blacks for: he charged that race and Hill's accusations had made him a victim; he accused the Judiciary Committee of engaging in the "high-tech lynching" of an accomplished African American (he used the tern "uppity black").[57]

The sensitivity that surrounded these charges clearly demonstrated that African Americans had indeed come a long way, for not even the mostly conservative Judiciary Committee denied Clarence Thomas the Supreme Court seat. Even more important was the fact that black conservatism had emerged as a serious political ideology in African America. Thomas was picked, as historian Kenneth O'Reilly pointed out, because "Bush wanted to make the court an arm of the presidency and guarantee that its justices would uphold the state against the citizens." But Thomas would also be symbolic of a new breed of African American intellectual and leader: one who would espouse conservatism and blend black nationalism with integration.[58]

Thus while Thomas was silent on the separatist rantings of the Nation of Islam, he advocated that black Americans should lift themselves up by their own bootstraps. Even more important was the fact that, despite the strong criticism that Thomas and other black conservatives received from liberals such as A. Leon Higginbotham and leftists such as Cornel West, there was a discernible shift in the ways in which blacks now viewed the political system.[59]

The collapse of a definable leftist movement, the improvement of the economy in the late 1990s, a new president who appeared to have

African American interests at heart, and the emergence of a neo-Black Renaissance enabled African American conservatives to signal that perhaps the time to move beyond race toward a color-blind society had arrived. Of all the above, it was the rise of new and vibrant cultural productions that created not only the possibilities for the black con-servatives' vision but also some critique of that vision and suggestions for more progressive alternatives.

4

POPULAR CULTURE
AND THE AFRICAN
AMERICAN
INTELLECTUAL
SEARCH FOR A
NEW AMERICAN
IDENTITY

In a bizarre set of circumstances, president pro tempore
Senator Douglass Dilman finds himself thrust into the
presidency of the United States. The Cold War crackles and domestic
peace is strained due to racial tensions.[1] Dilman's ascendancy to the
presidency can only exacerbate these national-international tensions.
Douglass Dilman, quiet and obscure, is black.

In *The Man,* a dramatic potboiler that used the backdrop of the
1960s Civil Rights movement and the emerging Black Power movement,
popular author Irving Wallace seized upon one fact that in most American minds, at that time, was utterly fantastical: an African American
as president of the United States. Wallace, whose heritage was Russian
Jewish and who was an avowed liberal, knew that a contrivance to
make a black man president had to be worked out in a thickly tangled
but nonetheless plausible and entertaining manner. The vice president
is dead; the president dies in a tragic accident overseas; and the Speaker
of the House dies on an operating table, thus leaving the presidency
to Douglass Dilman.

Once seen as a token for the late president's concerns for black rights,
Dilman is all but invisible to the white male political players. His becoming president not only sends shock waves throughout political
Washington but throws into bold visibility the deeply rooted racial
prejudice that afflicts the nation. Thus Irving Wallace's political potboiler was also meant to challenge white Americans' thinking about
race. But as thrilling, and some might say implausible, as his novel's
premise was, African American intellectuals/writers had mined some

of the most salient features of the book years before. Indeed Wallace's book could not have taken its shape had not Richard Wright written *Native Son* or, more closely to the main theme of invisibility, Ralph Ellison written *Invisible Man.*

When Wallace's *The Man* appeared, Ralph Ellison was bringing out his stunning and deeply probing book of essays, *Shadow and Act.* Twelve years after *Invisible Man,* Ellison put forth a series of essays written from the mid-1940s to the near present of the 1960s. The running thread was an attempt to dissect and understand the American racial sensibility. Having moved from the Far Left of his youth in the 1930s to a more liberal center in the late '40s and '50s, Ellison never shook off the strong feeling that African American nationalism was intricately bound up in American nationhood.[2]

Eschewing that form of black nationalism that embraced racial chauvinism, Ellison took an integrationist stance that would prefigure the values of the black and white youth of SNCC and, even later, the multiculturalism of the 1990s and the early twenty-first century. Ellison most certainly adhered to a cosmopolitanism that was open to all cultures of difference. His keen interest was in how the various cultures of difference (be they black, European, Jewish, or Native American) shaped American culture and society. In that sense, perhaps, his logical progenitor was Frederick Douglass, who outlined America as a "composite nation."[3]

Ellison also sought to outline and comprehend how race and identity in the fashioning of America was buried in complex layers at once psychological, social, economic, and political. Though *Invisible Man* and *Shadow and Act* embraced a liberal humanism that was more in line with the anticommunist liberal center then regnant in the 1960s, Ellison's deep leftist associations were not completely severed. Indeed, a strong argument has been made (and it is quite persuasive) that for all of Ellison's shift to the mainstream political center, it was his roots in and affiliations with leftist organizations and journals that formed the basis for his integrationist mode of thinking.[4]

Ellison's insistence on depoliticizing art as propaganda in no way diminished his desire to see political change take place for the improvement of African Americans. Art, for Ralph Ellison, was an individual enterprise at seeking the truth about American identity and its deep involvement with race. Ellison sought to stand apart from any group or political organization to fully see, understand, and explain the volatile, sometimes elastic, sometimes surreal landscape of American culture.

Invisible Man was the artistic novel of the truth about American identity and race. *Shadow and Act* was almost an academic exercise in laying out how *IM* evolved.[5]

By the mid-1960s, Ellison was recovering from the devastating loss of the work on his latest project in a house fire in New England. The new novel, which had become a matter of ongoing chatter among the black intelligentsia, young and old, was supposed to expand upon Ellison's search for the truth about America's identity. By the time of his death in 1994, Ellison had amassed over two thousand pages of text that, in a heavily edited form, was posthumously published as *Juneteenth* by his literary executor, John Callahan.[6] The novel displayed a rich tapestry and the promise of an even clearer exposition of the interplay of race, individualism, and communality that, to Ellison, comprised America. But there were gaps in this edited version that raised puzzling questions. While the entire manuscript would eventually see the light of publication, there were clear indications that black cultural and political activities of the late 1960s, '70s, and '80s weighed heavily on Ralph Ellison's quest to lay bare the truth about American identity.[7]

While Ralph Ellison found the historical roots of his ideas in the betrayal of African Americans at the end of Reconstruction, other African American writers in the late 1960s and '70s went back further and tapped into the era of slavery. Ellison probably would not have objected to this deeper excavation. After all, the American enterprise was intimately bound up with the enforced bondage of Africans. But there was a subtle black nationalism that ran through this oeuvre, especially if one looked at the stunning collection of remembrances in Julius Lester's *To Be a Slave* or the allegorical imagery of flight in Toni Morrison's *Song of Solomon*.[8] Lester's compendium sought to give voice to the millions of blacks enslaved throughout the South. More importantly, this book (which was cast as a work for young adults) legitimated the tradition of slave narratives undertaken by the Federal Writers Project in the thirties. Long ignored by the mainstream historical guild, Lester's work contributed to and heavily influenced the burgeoning field of slavery studies in the 1970s and '80s.[9]

While there was a black nationalist aura around these works, there was also a strong American cast to them. Toni Morrison's *Song of Solomon*, which was favorably compared to Ralph Ellison's *Invisible Man* in some quarters, used similar surrealistic and coded messages that adhered strongly to the liberal humanism of Ellison. Morrison clearly saw the "African" at the core of American culture and nation. In her Massey lectures at Harvard University in the early 1990s, she was explicit on this point: "Africanism is the vehicle by which the American self knows itself as not enslaved, but free; not repulsive, but desirable; not helpless, but licensed and powerful; not history-less, but historical; not damned, but innocent; not a blind accident of evolution, but a progressive fulfillment of destiny."[10] She was even more direct when she asserted, "The presence of black people is inherent, along with gender and family ties, in the earliest lessons every child is taught regarding his or her distinctiveness. Africanism is inextricable from the definition of Americanism from its origins on through its integrated or disintegrating twentieth century self" (65).

While these two passages bear the marks of an African American intellectual's semantical dance with Afrocentrism, closer examination suggests a stronger affiliation with Ralph Ellison's thinking or the pensive thought of James Baldwin. Morrison's attempt to tease out the layers of Africanness in the definition of American identity could only lead her to the same conclusion that Ellison arrived at; the core of American culture was buried by years of psychological guilt of whites who trafficked in human chattel and those whites who fought for the abolition of an otherwise profitable and nation-building enterprise. The fundamental difference between Morrison's, Lester's, and African American historian Leslie Owens's approach and Ellison's was perspective. The pull toward a black nationalist reading of history carried on so ably by Vincent Harding and Sterling Stuckey sought to situate American history through black eyes and voices. Ralph Ellison moved to see that same history as an amalgam of black and white.[11]

In doing so, Ellison adopted an approach that reached out to the white literary canon (particularly the nineteenth-century writers Herman Melville, Henry David Thoreau, and Ellison's namesake, Ralph Waldo Emerson) to uncover the Negro identity within it. Toni Morrison and those previously mentioned, caught up in the slavery studies paradigm of black slave cultural autonomy in the 1977os and '80s, concentrated more on the immersion of blacks in a harsh white supremacist society. Thus in Toni Morrison's acclaimed novel *Beloved*, the only adequate response to this oppression is the dissolution of any relationship to the United States. By the mid-1990s, as a neo–Black Renaissance bloomed amid the media-labeled "culture wars," this black nationalist/Afrocentric approach was softening. Ralph Ellison's belief was, as African American intellectual historian Jerry Gafio Watts has stated, that "blacks have been seminal creators of American culture and America has been a profound influence on the creation of black culture. In effect, black and white Americans have lived in antagonistic cooperation." This was now being vindicated in a number of areas in popular culture, whether literary, cinematic, musical, or even in the emergence of black comic strips.[12]

In literature this was clearly seen in Julius Lester's acclaimed novel *And All Our Wounds Forgiven*. A finalist for a National Book Award in 1994, the work was a meditation on and reevaluation of the Civil Rights–Black Power era and therefore comported well with Ralph Ellison's ideas regarding the multilayered complexities of America and the American identity.[13] The story is told through the eyes of a number of participants in the movement some thirty years later and overseen by the choruslike voice of the movement's main leader, John Calvin Marshall. While there are similarities to Ellison's *Invisible Man*, *And All Our Wounds Forgiven* stands apart from *IM* in its attempt to weigh the moral, spiritual, and political implications of the Civil Rights movement as it struggled to bring about true equality for blacks and racial harmony and healing for the nation. In Lester's view (voiced through John Calvin Marshall), the movement had good intentions that had tragic consequences.

Marshall recalls a speech given early on in the movement on the steps of the Congress in Washington, D.C.: "I come here today to plead with the white people of this nation for freedom. But I do not come to plead for Freedom for the Negro. No! It is the white man's freedom that I seek. . . . The Negro cannot be free until you stop being white. Only when you stop being white will you stop seeing us as black. Only then will you see that you have been wounded by this disfiguring notion of race more deeply than we" (56). Marshall's eloquent, if not provocative, speech causes the *Washington Post* and the *New York Times* to applaud, stating, as Marshall puts it, that they "speculated that a run for the presidency might not succeed but it would certainly make a more honest man out of jfk" (56).

Thus Lester, who participated in both SNCC and the Black Power movement before becoming a counterculture critic, moved far beyond the potboiling entertainment of Irving Wallace's *The Man*. And yet Lester clearly seemed to have recognized the "omni-Americaness" of Ralph Ellison and James Baldwin as he moved to imagine the true nature of the American identity.[14] But *And All Our Wounds Forgiven* is also an examination of what happens when the movement loses sight of its goals. Here Lester does not hold back and comes closest to an Ellisonian reading of what history has produced:

> I have wondered if the real worth of the civil rights movement was not interracial sex. Do not misunderstand. I am not deriding the passage of the 1964 civil rights act or the 1965 voting rights act. I am not dishonoring the memories of all of us who died. But if social change is the transformation of values, then the civil rights movement did not fulfill itself. There has not been any diminution in the ethic of white supremacy. Instead racism has added legions of *black* adherents, making America an integrated society in a way I never dreamed. Our racial suspicions and hatreds have made us one nation. (71)

This gloomy critique was fitting for a black intelligentsia and leadership that, since the late 1970s, appeared to have lost its moral compass. But Lester's ultimate message in this novel is that there must be a move toward healing and remembering what the Civil Rights movement really accomplished. In an interview in the *Forward* shortly after the publication of *And All Our Wounds Forgiven*, Lester made it clear what he thought the Civil Rights movement did:

> It really has not been fully acknowledged and appreciated that the civil rights movement was a success. The civil rights movement set out to end legal segregation and ensure the rights of blacks to vote—and we succeeded.
>
> It's also been totally lost that the civil rights movement was a racially integrated movement—it was not an all black movement. . . . It's really the only interracial movement that we've seen in the 20th century.[15]

For Lester, then, racial healing and harmony must begin with an acknowledgement of the successes of the Civil Rights movement and a regaining of a "generosity of spirit among many African Americans who do not recognize that there were white people who did care and do care now."[16]

If the area of literature, both popular and high-minded, grappled earnestly with the meanings of blackness and the situation of race in the late twentieth century, there was also the realization that the American obsession with race could easily become blurred with commercialization and consumption. The roles that commercialization and consumption play in enhancing or undermining black cultural production has long proved to be a vexatious problem for African American intellectuals. W. E. B. Du Bois tried to formulate black culture as a political and propagandistic program for black civil rights during the Harlem

Renaissance. In the late 1930s and '40s, writers and intellectuals such as Richard Wright, Ralph Ellison, and Langston Hughes saw literature and music and black folk culture shaped by industrialization and urbanization as pathways to understanding black culture and its integral role in shaping American society and culture.[17]

Richard Wright's "Blueprint for Negro Writing" represented a black intellectual effort at harnessing the best of Western civilization's literary examinations of humanity's problems to the folk consciousness of African Americans. While Wright's essay emanated from his association with the Left (in particular the Communist party), it was also inspired by an independent stance on artistic writing coupled with an understanding of an undercurrent of black nationalism within the psyche of the black masses. Ralph Ellison shared Richard Wright's vision on a literary level for the most part but filtered it through the cultural lens of jazz (and later bebop). Ellison also moved further from the dogmatic realism favored by the Left to a more humanistic, even existentialist/ psychological rendering of African Americans. Like Langston Hughes, Ellison saw black cultural production moving from a rapidly declining rural folk expression to a modern, industrialized, rhythmic improvisation that was signified by jazz. Added to this was a cosmopolitanism that crossed boundaries to include the analyses of such intellectuals as Afro-Caribbeans Oliver C. Cox, George Padmore, and C. L. R. James and African Kwame Nkrumah.[18]

The task was to understand the nationality of African Americans as a duality: at once American and yet set apart through the wrenching experience of slavery and the ideology of race. This "dual consciousness" (which obviously harkened back to Du Bois's conceptualization of the black American condition) was further complicated by certain segments of the dominant society's willingness to appropriate black cultural productions for entertainment and profit.[19]

Elite whites could indulge themselves in viewing black art or listening to jazz singers and musicians even as these cultural productions laid bare a world where black people were lynched (Billie Holliday's "Strange Fruit") or caught up in the industrialized frenzy of the modern urban landscape (Duke Ellington's "A Train" or Dizzy Gillespie's bebop and later Charlie Parker and John Coltrane). The struggle to make these black cultural productions forums for political activity in order to tear down racial barriers and liberate black people proved to be highly elusive. All too often they were yoked to rising liberal anticommunist thought that sought to demonstrate to a Cold War–driven world that the United States was a truly free, fair democracy. Thus for every Langston Hughes or Zora Neale Hurston who lauded black folk culture there was an E. Franklin Frazier who disdained it and called for eventual full integration. And for every Ralph Ellison who found riches in the cultural expression of jazz, there was an African American elite who was embarrassed if not contemptuous of jazz's influence.[20]

The dilemma would persist throughout the twentieth century, flaring up as movements for black liberation emerged and declined. The Civil Rights movement was preceded by a rich black cultural creation of rhythm and blues, which contained a certain black folk/nationalist sensibility. Confined to segregated playlists and homegrown record labels such as Stax/Volt or Chess Records, rhythm and blues artists created a music that easily resonated in the segregated enclaves of the South and even in the black inner-city neighborhoods of the North.[21]

Commercialization blurred, if not blunted, the political force of these cultural productions. Ahmet Ertegun and Jerry Wexler's formation of Atlantic Records showcased some of the most brilliant black artists ranging from Aretha Franklin to Otis Redding to Isaac Hayes. While many black artists honed their music in response to the charged and changing political atmosphere of the 1950s and '60s, black pop was implicitly political in its commercial move to cross over and reach young white audiences. Performers such as Sam Cooke of Mississippi and Jackie Wilson of Detroit led the way.[22]

By the time of the March on Washington, the peak of the early Civil Rights movement, the biracial crossover found many black listeners, in and out of the movement, playing the music of Joan Baez, Bob Dylan, and Bobby Darin, as well as Peter, Paul, and Mary. African American intellectuals immersed themselves in the "new jazz" sounds of Ornette Coleman, Cecil Taylor, and Charles Mingus. These musicians imbued their music with a defiance at the received wisdom of Western civilization (read white) musical standards (Ward, 304–7).

But it was Berry Gordy's Motown records that best exemplified the full-blown commercialization and consumption of black popular musical/cultural productions. Gordy, in many respects, was representative of that duality in black American consciousness with which so many African American intellectuals grappled. Working with talented black youth in Detroit's housing projects, Gordy had little trouble finding and maintaining several groups of outstanding acts. What was particularly fascinating about Gordy's enterprise was his fervent attempt to integrate the black nationality more fully into American consciousness. In order to do so, his groups were not as raw or steeped in the rural/urban black culture of the South. Gordy's groups were more polished, and Gordy was conscientious about reaching a wider audience regardless of race, region, or even generation. Thus while he may have used race as an initial point of solidarity, his business acumen and ingenious building of the Motown Sound eschewed any black nationalist sentiment that was an undercurrent in some groups associated with Stax/Volt or with the soul singer considered the "hardest working man in show business": James Brown.[23] Berry Gordy's acts were polished, upbeat, good-looking, and ready for entry into middle-class America. The crossover appeal may not have been overtly politically motivated, but the effect fit. And more, it was in keeping with the notion of black cultural productions constructed as vehicles for entertaining whites. A crucial difference from activists was that Gordy profited from his experience. It was clearly a black entrepreneurial enterprise that demonstrated that black individuals could reap material success and advancement from the racial group's creations and reproductions. Motown spawned such successful groups as Smokey Robinson and the Miracles, the Four Tops, Tami Terrell and Marvin Gaye, the Supremes (later Diana Ross and the Supremes), and perhaps one of the most successful single acts and certainly the most widely accepted in white and black America, Stevie Wonder. The musical writing talents of Eddie and Brad Holland and Lamont Dozier girded these groups and others in Gordy's stable (Ward, 263).

What was most intriguing about these artists was the trajectory that they took as the Black Power movement overtook the Civil Rights movement. Black Power/nationalism's insistence on a unifying black cultural enterprise threatened the crossover appeal that had been ridden for most of the 1960s. Those black artists in Motown who ventured forthrightly into the political realm did so cautiously. The Temptations' "Ball of Confusion" was a testament to the social commentary that had come from the polished soul singers of years before. Marvin Gaye produced a stunning concept album that was not only rhythmically in keeping with the Motown brand but also laced with a black nationalist sentiment that commented on the plight of America's black ghettoes. It was an album that was equally in tune with the counterculture.

It was the rise of the anti–Vietnam War movement, the seemingly endless urban rebellions in the inner cities during the summers of the 1960s, the increasing radicalization of the Black Panther party (which certainly was not as separatist as other black nationalist groups), and the flowering of the black arts movement that caused splits and fissures within black cultural production. As mentioned before, black pop groups that strove for crossover audiences that embraced racial harmony now found themselves making social commentary regarding the black condition in the urban areas of the nation. For artists such as Edwin Starr ("War") or the Temptations ("Ball of Confusion"), or even later, Stevie Wonder (whose albums *Talking Book* and *Inner-visions* remain classics), there was still an earnest attempt to hold fast to an integrationist appeal (Ward, 346, 363).

But they were no match for a newer crop of black artists who took the ideas of community, individuality, and racial harmony to a different level. A prime example was Jimi Hendrix, rhythm and blues guitarist from the West Coast who went to England and was exposed to white progressive rock. When Hendrix returned to the United States in 1967, his integrated group, the Jimi Hendrix Experience, was poised to rise as a signature icon of counterculture rock. Though he had solid roots in black musical traditions, Hendrix's core audience would be mostly white and therefore he seemed cut off from the black world. His influence on progressive white American rockers from Stephen Stills to Janis Joplin to groups like Crosby, Stills, Nash, and Young demonstrated how black cultural productions could shape the American popular cultural landscape.[24]

That pattern would continue through the 1970s with groups like Sly and the Family Stone and the rise of disco. Disco's appeal was certainly commercial, but it also emanated from a coalescing of Latin music, rhythm and blues, and gay aesthetics. It exposed a newer level of crossover appeal and inclusion that reflected the post–Civil Rights era or what Nelson George, the black music critic and commentator, perceptively calls "post-soul."[25]

For George, post-soul was clearly the development of a new black cultural environment from the mid-1970s through the decade of the 1980s. As he put it, "Post-soul is my short hand to describe a time when America attempted to absorb the victories, failures, and ambiguities that resulted from the soul years. The post-soul years have witnessed an unprecedented acceptance of black people in the public life of America. . . . Unfortunately all that progress has not been as beneficial to the black masses as was anticipated in the '60s" (ix).

The linkages to the 1930s with their talk of class issues cannot be lost here. Indeed as the 1970s ended and throughout the 1980s, the emergence of the largest professional black middle class exerted tremendous pressure politically, enhanced the economic status of that class, and raised new questions regarding racial identity particularly, and identity formation in the United States generally. It was one of the sadder ironies, however, that the class analyses of the younger Turks of the 1930s (Abram Harris, E. Franklin Frazier, Ralph Bunche, to name but a few) would now be in contention with moralistic claims for equality and individualism. And to make matters even more complicated, the ideas surrounding racial formations and what it meant to be black were undergoing changes that even black intellectuals and commentators had difficulty keeping up with. Again Nelson George made the apt observation that "by decade's end [meaning the 1970s], 'black' itself, as a verbal identification of race, would be, if not replaced, at least challenged or reinterpreted by the introduction of a new phrase. In fact the definition of blackness would be in play in the '80s with terms like 'buppie,' 'b-boy,' 'BAP,' 'underclass,' 'womanist,' and 'Afrocentricity' entering the lexicon. Some of these terms were sepia-tinted versions of white reality; others slang terms and academic inventions that captured new identities."[26]

For the record, "sepia-tinted versions of white reality" were "yuppie" (young urban professional) as opposed to "buppie" (reflecting the new black middle class), "BAP" (black American princess) as opposed to "JAP" (Jewish American Princess), which implied an ethnic quality and, again, a recognition of the arrival of the black middle class into mainstream America. "B-boy" (beat-boy) was hip-hop slang that throughout the 1980s and into the '90s would change as rap music became a commercial fixture in American popular culture. "Underclass" was an academic invention that sought to explain, sociologically if not economically, those left behind in the nation's inner cities as the professional black middle class formed enclaves (either suburban or urban) of their own. Significantly, the culture of the underclass would fuel the rise of hip-hop as an academic enterprise as well as a cultural production. However fluid identities became in the 1980s and '90s, there was an inherent tension between improvisational identity based in past and present historical experiences and time-worn notions of racial essentialism.

Thus "Afrocentricity" played off of race essentialism even as it sought to provide a foundation for middle-class blacks to feel and be authentically black. The fervent attempts by educators such as Molefi Asante Kete (who coined the term "Afrocentricity"), Leonard Jeffries, Asa Hilliard, and Frances Cress Welsing to solidify an identity and offer a critique of Western civilization's racialist assumptions struck an emotional chord with a black middle class that was part of what Henry Louis Gates Jr. termed the "cross-over generation" from Jim Crow over the bridge of integration to mainstream success.[27]

Yet it was questionable how well this intellectual construction could stand up to the scrutiny of those African American intellectuals who not only critiqued the race essentialist basis of Afrocentricity but were more animated about understanding the rapidly changing terrain of racial identity formation. An example would be the construct of "womanist," which started from a literary activist vantage point. Alice Walker, formerly of SNCC and a critically acclaimed novelist, coined the term in the early 1980s as part of her revival of the literary legacy of Zora Neale Hurston. Womanist theory ended up being a crucial theoretical tool in the building of academic black feminism. More generally, it served as a corrective not only to Afrocentrism's race essentialism but to its tendencies toward dismissing the importance that sex, gender, and class play in creating identity. Walker's efforts were presented to a wider audience with the release of her provocative novel *The Color Purple*.[28]

But it was the updating, as it were, of Du Bois's double-consciousness formulation of the black condition that was made in the early twentieth century that grasped black intellectuals so tenaciously. In a period that witnessed the full installation of not only a conservative administration led by Ronald Reagan but also an ideological shift in how African Americans and the whole question of cultural identity were composed, there arose two competing visions of black culture extracted from the "culture wars" that actually had an integral racial composition. One vision, put forth by white intellectuals such as Charles Murray and George Gilder, played on the theme of a pathological culture among inner-city African Americans. The culprits were the welfare state, the lack of responsible behavior and morals of the young, and the constant evasion of responsibility through claims of victimization due to institutional racism. The 1980s and '90s black conservatives' fine tuning of the thinking of earlier black conservatives such as Thomas Sowell walked a curiously integrationist path, as they not only sided with white conservative assessments of African American culture but also accused white liberals and radicals of playing the race card to the detriment of black people, whether poor or well off. Thus spoke Shelby Steele in the early years of the twenty-first century: "Today in America there is no moral relativism around racism, no sophisticated public sentiment that recasts racism as a mere 'quirk' of character. . . . Race simply replaced sex as the primary focus of America's moral seriousness."[29]

Steele's implication is that all moral relativism is wrong, a standard trope during these conservative years. Race becomes a "quirk" and sexual activity in public office (a direct allusion to the President Clinton–Monica Lewinsky debacle) an "indiscretion." Aside from a display of intellectual confusion, Steele demonstrated a vast lack of understanding of the historical context and complexity of race matters.

In the same vein, John McWhorter, a younger black conservative intellectual from Philadelphia, trained as a linguist but recruited into the conservative tent of the early twenty-first century, blames all of the woes of poor and middle-class blacks on the promiscuous years of the 1960s and the radical paternalism of white liberals and radicals. McWhorter summarized his first book, *Losing the Race: Self-Sabotage in America,* as "a book contending that 'black America is currently caught in certain ideological holding patterns'—chief among them being the ideology of permanent victimhood—and that there today are much more serious barriers to black well-being than is white racism."[30]

This brief summary can easily be called "blaming the victim." But a more nuanced question would be to ask how it is that African America has the largest black middle class of all time and yet there is still a disproportionately large pool of impoverished black people? Henry Louis Gates Jr. has pointed out that there are now two black Americas and the division grows wider.[31]

But John McWhorter wanted to blame black culture and "lowered standards," as well as "how rarely black professors who enter public discourse permitted themselves to stray from ritualized tribal plaints." This was standard conservative and neoconservative thinking from the late 1980s throughout the '90s. The foundation for this line of thought came from Allan Bloom's screed *The Closing of the American Mind.* Cultural degradation, moral relativism, and the dumbing down of education, all legacies of the 1960s, contributed to the unraveling of the social fabric.[32]

The drumbeat intensified in the 1990s as Dinesh D'Sousa, a young Asian Indian, groomed in the conservative manners of the *Dartmouth Review* and, later, the American Enterprise Institute, wrote *The End of Racism,* a book playing off Daniel Bell's classic sociological commentary *The End of Ideology.* D'Sousa's target, of course, was race. In his rereading of African American history, it was important to show that blacks owned slaves and moral relativism was started by Du Bois. D'Sousa defended Charles Murray and Richard Herrnstein's 1992 book on race, intelligence, and genetics, *The Bell Curve:* in order for blacks to improve their situation, they must learn the ways of western culture and realize that in the twenty-first century there is the end of racism.[33]

The most spirited attack on these works by conservative African American intellectuals and those white intellectuals sympathetic to what they regarded as "racial realism" was put forth by a group of scholars headed by Troy Duster, sociologist and grandson of Ida B. Wells-Barnett. Duster and his team assembled a critique that put forward not only a surgical deconstruction of the modern conservative paradigm on race but also encapsulated the alternative vision of what the new American identity could be. Certainly one thing that had to be dispensed with was the ongoing attempt, in the face of the historical achievements in civil rights going back to the 1930s, to whitewash race.[34] The group cites several major reasons for undertaking their study:

> We . . . know that demographic changes beginning in the last quarter of the twentieth century seriously complicate the meaning of race and racism. As large numbers of Asians and Latinos move into America's major urban areas, the politics of and economics of race are no longer represented in black and white. Old alliances based on race have been replaced by new multiracial coalitions. As racial intermarriages increase, the very meaning of race has been entangled in ways that were once inconceivable. And with the development of black cultural and athletic icons, blackness has been transformed from a badge of oppression into an image that is desired and emulated. (M. Brown, x)

To this new view of how America and American identity have been transformed, the authors forthrightly tackle the question of why we continue to see race in black and white. They state that they must deal with this issue because "the conservative consensus on race . . . is mostly constructed around the relationship between black and white. Thus, if we are to seriously engage and scrutinize this development, we need to address the issues it raises" (x).

The authors recognized that even though there is a new formation of identity in the United States that is overtaking the binary notion of race, "the black/white binary persists as a feature of everyday life and is crucial to the commonsense understanding of racism" (x). And that is because the embedded conception of "whiteness" continues to define who is and who is not American. These authors, representative loosely of a multiculturalist and leftist view, wanted not only to dissect the continuing dilemma of race but also understand the ongoing development of a new multicultural America. To that end, while their work looked at the standard social science indices of education, wealth, poverty, political advancement, and organization, they saw much cause for hope as well as concern.

However, the main areas of cultural production, the focus of this chapter's consideration, are sorely lacking. For despite any sociological promises that could be brought forth, there were also deep concerns for what had not been accomplished. Historically, in times of tumultuous administrations when ideological tensions ran high, black cultural productions fermented and presented challenging visions and critiques. The Harlem Renaissance during the 1920s was one such period; the Popular Front of the 1930s was yet another and, perhaps, more important one, given the legacies extracted from the New Deal's nurturing of African American intellectuals/writers such as Richard Wright, Ralph Ellison, and Shirley Graham Du Bois.

With the end of World War II and America's entrance into the Cold War, black cultural productions once again began to build up steam. If there was political recognition among liberals of white supremacy and Jim Crow segregation as ideological obstacles in projecting the United States to the world as the foremost free nation, African American intellectuals waged a serious struggle culturally throughout the 1950s and 1960s to demonstrate the integral role that African Americans had contributed in shaping the country: for example, the writings of James Baldwin, who wrote about an America that was much in the vein of Ralph Ellison, while the plays (such as *A Raisin in the Sun*) and activism of Lorraine Hansberry saw the black struggle as not only to be free but to reshape the United States into a truly integrated society. Meanwhile African American intellectuals and artists embraced the liberation struggles emerging in Africa.[35]

And yet the backlash that came in the late 1960s after the "long hot summers" and the rise of an angry black nationalist movement that wanted total liberation of black people from a nation condemned as corrupt, imperialist, and oppressive saw even more black cultural productions. Some of these creations reflected the black nationalist ethos of the black arts movement. Still other creative efforts pushed into the mainstream movies, television, and the print media, pressing new images, sounds, and words of African Americans ready to take the United States into a new racial and social landscape.[36]

Despite the lamentations of black intellectuals such as Cornel West in the late 1980s that there was no African American intelligentsia to challenge the rollback of the accomplishments of the 1960s, black cultural productions, in or out of the mainstream, had become a neo-Renaissance of blackness. In many ways similar to the Harlem Renaissance, this new cultural flowering was marked by the richly rewarding appearances of black women writers such as Alice Walker, Toni Morrison, Maya Angelou, and June Jordan, who were known from the 1960s and '70s. A cadre of black women intellectuals such as Hazel Carby, Patricia Hill Collins, bell hooks, Patricia Williams, and Beverly Guy-Sheftall now joined them.[37]

With the rise of hip-hop in the 1970s, the ground was prepared for a fusion of a political and cultural reading and critique of American racial identity and relations. Again a new crop of African American intellectuals, most of whom were academicians and beneficiaries of the Civil Rights movement of the 1960s and '70s, rose to visibility as explainers and critics of the way things were going on racially in the country, which again was in the grips of ideological tension as conservatives, social, religious, or traditional, tightened their grip in the political and diplomatic arenas.

For those who feared that the Civil Rights achievements of the previous generation were in serious jeopardy one could only concur with Nikhil Pal Singh's assessment: "The now widely held view that any race-based amelioration constitutes a form of reverse discrimination indicates that the public effort to secure social, civil and political redress for racially aggrieved communities has reached an historic impasse, if not an end."[38] Nonetheless, the cultural productions of African Americans moved steadily forward, and when seen in conjunction with the work of Troy Duster and his group, it can be concluded that serious changes were occurring. One of the most intriguing looks at the new developments of race could be found in graphic comics and daily comic strips.

Daily comic strips and political cartoons have been a deeply embedded part of American popular culture since the nation's beginnings. Political cartoons in newspapers and magazines have measured the pulse of the nation's attitudes and emotions about a wide range of topics and events. It certainly was no different with regard to race. One only has to think of Thomas Nast's series of political cartoons in *Harper's Weekly* depicting the emancipation of African Americans (sympathetically rendered) to the tension-filled events and ultimate betrayal of multiracial democracy during Reconstruction (not always sympathetically rendered).[39]

But political cartoons aside, popular comic strips in newspapers began their heyday in the late nineteenth century and were a distinctly

urban phenomenon. In the rapidly growing industrialized cities, immigrant populations crowded in enclaves and took in all manners of
entertainment. Comics reflected (and reinforced) the diversity of these
congested cities. Racially, African Americans were seen, especially
in light of segregation and vicious marginalization, as the ultimate
"other." Many, if not all, immigrant groups measured themselves on
a register that found African Americans on the bottom. And so it was
with the comic strips of American city newspapers.[40]

By the 1920s and '30s, the rise of newspaper syndicates and national
distribution networks was firmly set. The content of comics as read by
the vast majority of Americans presented entertainment that appealed
to an increasingly consumer-oriented culture. Given that comic strips
were an urban-based cultural creation, the trafficking in ethnic stereotypes became so common that it was hard to see how the commodifi-
cation of these sometimes vicious stereotypes masked real changes in
the diversity and, ultimately, power sharing of various ethnic groups in
the cities. While ethnic stereotypes in comic strips were used to mask
subtle or not so subtle shifts in urban demographics, the representation
of African Americans remained a constant. Often grotesquely drawn
and voiced in crude dialect, the presence of blacks was meant to be
entertainment and at the same time reinforce their inferior status. The
only places where African Americans were presented in a positive light
was in black newspapers.

Black newspapers such as the *Chicago Defender, Pittsburgh Courier,
Philadelphia Tribune,* and *Amsterdam News* carried comic strips of
cartoon commentaries that were humorous and entertaining as well
as laden with messages of uplift and hope for the advancement of the
race. Focused mainly on entertaining and inculcating valuable lessons
for newly arrived migrants to the city, black newspaper comics differed
from their mainstream counterparts in presenting African Americans
as human beings trying to make it in a modern world like everyone else.

In the 1930s, during the Depression, the *Philadelphia Independent*
carried a comic strip that highlighted these components while at the
same time presenting a message heralding bourgeois and consumerist
values. It was also a rarity for black newspapers, as it was an action
adventure strip. Black cartoonist Branford's *The Jones Family* was a
precursor to the more robust action comics developed in the 1990s by
DC Comics under the black-run Milestone label.[41]

In the post–World War II era, comic strips and comic books changed
dramatically. As the United States emerged as a world power, comic

strips were affected by and, in turn, reflected shifts in ideology and expanded forms of consumer culture. Ideologically, the rise of liberal anticommunism in response to the Soviet Union's attempt to align itself with oppressed and developing nations was reflected in comic strips and books that trumpeted the virtues and values of the American way of life. In many regards, race was barely visible, and again it was in black magazines such as John H. Johnson's *Negro Digest* or *Sepia* where cartoonists such as Oliver W. "Ollie" Harrington would subtly and sometimes humorously critique the order of the day by attacking segregation and race prejudice.[42]

The Civil Rights era, which found renewed focus and intensity after World War II, also inevitably found reflection in comics. But efforts to integrate African Americans into mainstream comics would continue running into roadblocks of deeply entrenched racial stereotypes and white supremacist attitudes until the 1980s. The most visible images of blacks were connected to strips that featured Africa as a main location. Though not as grotesquely rendered as in the past, African natives were nonetheless cast as barbarians who needed white guidance or control.[43]

One instance, actually a first, of a black character of respectability making it into a nationally syndicated comic strip was in Leonard Starr's New York–based melodramatic strip *Mary Perkins, on Stage*. The character was presented as an expert voice coach and was modeled on Phil Moore, a black music coach and friend of Starr's. The strip appeared in 1961 and the Chicago Tribune Syndicate faced heavy pressure from Southern and Northern papers that objected to the storyline. The character was in the story briefly but despite Leonard Starr's courageous attempt at integrating his strip, it would not be until the 1990s that American newspapers and the comic book industry would see a thorough and intriguing integration abound.[44]

Mainstream newspapers brought black comic strips that focused mostly on middle-class families and their children as they faced humorous situations. These "color-blind" strips were black only in regard to the way the characters were drawn. There was no crude dialect or overexaggerated facial features or body types. Comics like Nemstrong's *Jump Start* or Greg's *Luann* presented a post–Civil Rights black experience that was more in the vein of the hit television show of the 1980s, *The Cosby Show*. These innocuous strips began in the mid-1990s just as the action comics of Milestone/DC were taking off for young black readers (mostly male). But in 1998, a comic strip arrived of a humorous, entertaining, and provocative intellectual caliber.[45]

Aaron McGruder is a representative of the post–Civil Rights/integration/Black Power eras. A graduate from the University of Maryland with degrees in African American studies and communication, McGruder took a long and full measure of the racial progress of the last generation. Heading to Los Angeles, he developed a comic strip that he had begun while an undergraduate. *The Boondocks* first appeared in the white-owned hip-hop magazine *The Source*. By 1999, it was in national syndication in hundreds of daily newspapers where the American populace was daily treated to a sidesplitting but hard-hitting dose of the state of racial reality in the nation.[46]

Though he situated himself on the left, McGruder never flinched from making harsh criticisms of liberal attitudes among blacks and whites. He poured heavy critical heat on aspects of hip-hop culture while extolling the virtues of the bygone days of Civil Rights and Black Power. This was clearly seen in his characters. The strip centered on two young black brothers, Huey and Riley Freeman, who had moved into an integrated suburb outside their South Side Chicago neighborhood. The setups are brilliantly raw and illuminating takes on how race is lived in New Millennium America.

The change is hard for the youngsters; they live with their grandfather who represents an "old school" civil rights liberal who has managed to cross over into middle-class comfort (he owns the suburban house the boys reside in). Grandpa tries to inculcate the same middle-class values that have always been the archetype of the black comic strips in the black newspapers of the past. But McGruder goes beyond this and nicely juxtaposes those values with the reality of an America whose identity formation has been positively (negatively?) shaped by the events since the close of World War II and the Cold War. Here he deals with the effects of a postintegration period that saw a rise in multiculturalism and an increase in biracial identity.

In the character of Jasmine, a delightfully precocious daughter of a professionally successful interracial couple (father is black, mother is white, both are lawyers), McGruder shows how racial identity becomes confused with liberal beliefs in American individualism. Huey, ever the revolutionary socialist black nationalist (much like his namesake, Huey Newton of the Black Panthers), constantly goads Jasmine into claiming and rejoicing in her "Nubian" blackness. He scolds her father, Tom Du Bois (a hilarious jab at the idea of "Uncle Tom" and the aloofness of W. E. B. Du Bois), for not providing Jasmine with a better understanding of her black racial self and past. When Huey is not trying to sort out and straighten out the entangled thickets of racial identity, he is trying to keep his brother, Riley, a young gangsta wannabe, from being swallowed up in hip-hop violence and misogynist behavior.

This was the first nationally syndicated comic strip that looked at America's racial face straight on and exposed it. To read *The Boondocks* (or view the television show that premiered on the "Adult Swim" Comedy Network cable channel) is to understand how deeply race is embedded in American culture. It is a fresh portal that one can walk through and know that its connections to the past will not be severed or betrayed. And here many thanks must go to those valiant black intellectuals of the 1930s and '40s, no matter what their political leanings. From the fierce intensity of the leftist/liberal writings of Richard Wright, Ralph Ellison, Langston Hughes, Shirley Graham Du Bois, Langston Hughes, and later James Baldwin and Lorraine Hansberry to the sharp satirical and individualistic stances of George S. Schuyler and Zora Neale Hurston, they have all shaped in some manner Aaron McGruder's understanding of what has been wrought in a twenty-first-century American identity.

The Boondocks, as a vital black cultural production, is also a clear indication of where African American intellectuals and the nation are heading. What are the vital questions? Can the visibility and viability of black intellectual dialogue be reinvigorated, if not sustained?

[5] A NEW CENTURY AND NEW CHALLENGES: THE VISIBILITY OF AFRICAN AMERICAN INTELLECTUALS AND THE CONSTRUCTION OF DIASPORIC DIVERSITY

H istory is not marked by the man-made devices of generations, decades, or centuries. The imprint of a new century or millennium may occur well before or well into the artificially set parameters of a given time. Thus, the beginnings of America's ascendancy as a world power began in the late nineteenth century and perhaps peaked in the late twentieth century. Likewise, the struggles of African Americans for freedom and equality in a nation they helped to forge culturally, economically, and politically have ebbed and flowed from the signing of the Emancipation Proclamation in the middle of the Civil War to the startling reminder of racism's tenacity (and viciousness) in the aftermath of Hurricane Katrina in 2005.

The visibility of African American intellectuals as seriously considered voices in the public discourse has also defied neat historical delineation. From the time of Frederick Douglass and Alexander Crummell to the late-nineteenth- and twentieth-century writings of Booker T. Washington and W. E. B. Du Bois, African American intellectuals were listened to by white elites and educated blacks, but overall their public intellectual stances were often marginalized or pigeonholed by the specter of flawed race relations.[1]

African American women intellectuals fared worse, even though they offered incisive insights into how race, class, and gender intertwined into a rope that not only threatened to strangle any advancement for African Americans but also continued to sink the nation into the deadly quicksand of racism and white supremacy. Pauline Hopkins, Anna Julia Cooper, Alice Dunbar Nelson, and Ida B. Wells-Barnett were all precursors of the African American women intellectuals in the twentieth and twenty-first centuries. Their work, as much overshadowed by that of male intellectuals as by the blinders of racism in the dominant white society, laid the foundations for the more visible black feminist theories of the late twentieth and twenty-first centuries. Black feminist intellectuals such as bell hooks, Patricia Williams, June Jordan, Alice Walker, and Patricia Hill Collins to name but a few built from the foundations of their foresisters and took a more visible and equal place beside their male counterparts.[2]

Adding to the visibility and strength of African American intellectuals has been the fruitful emergence of what may be called a diasporic intelligentsia that includes black intellectuals from Africa, the Caribbean, and England. The work of these intellectuals has invigorated African American intellectuals' understanding of race and power not only in historical and national contexts but also, and perhaps more importantly, globally. The theoretical structures developed by Afro-British scholars such as Stuart Hall, Paul Gilroy, and Hazel Carby have stirred a reexamination of how race is formed and what new meanings and shapes it will take in the twenty-first century. Likewise, the infusion of new analyses of gender relations between black males and females has not only spurred controversy but generated an intensity in the search to understand and elaborate on racial identity in a rapidly changing world of diversity.[3]

It is no wonder then that in the 1990s there was a reappearance of the Africa-based journal of ideas *Transition*. Formed in the early 1960s, the journal was revived by Henry Louis Gates Jr. and Wole Soyinka and quickly rose throughout the decade to become a leading platform for black intellectuals to discuss and examine the place of race and diasporic diversity as a new century was dawning.[4]

There were other attempts at making black intellectuals visible in public forums. Randall Kennedy, a former law clerk for Thurgood Marshall and professor of law at Harvard University, put out an intriguing intellectual journal titled *Reconstruction*. This project sought to engage, if not confront, some of the thornier issues that faced African

America and did so through inviting white as well as black intellectuals to debate topics ranging from affirmative action in higher education to reflections on the Holocaust, and a reexamination of important events in African American history that should be incorporated back into American history.[5]

What was most interesting about these intellectual venues was where they emanated from. African American intellectuals of the late twentieth century were ensconced in predominately white educational institutions ("PWIs") instead of the historically black colleges and universities ("HBCUs"). As such, much of the visibility of these black scholars was due to their affiliation at such high-profile research universities as Harvard, Yale, Stanford, Princeton, Columbia, the University of Chicago, and the University of Michigan. This visibility, in turn, enabled new cadres of black public intellectuals who appeared regularly in mainstream print media and on television news and talk programs addressing issues pertaining to race and its perennial dilemma in the nation.

In 1997, when President William Jefferson Clinton commissioned an Initiative on Race, he appointed the distinguished African American historian John Hope Franklin, as its head. The initiative arose out of a series of dinner seminars held by Vice President Al Gore and signaled an earnest effort by President Clinton to come up with answers as to what race would mean in the coming century. There were certainly ample enough reasons for this move. There was a profound mistrust by African Americans of the contentions of whites. The continued volatile politicization of affirmative action was one such contention. Then there were the code words that masked racist sentiments and the media representations on reality programs such as *Cops* that presented African Americans in the age-old paradigm of cultural pathology. And despite the demise of segregation and an overt culture that saw black people as an amorphous mass that was more often than not rendered invisible, there now appeared more subtle but nonetheless irritating and humiliating forms of race blindness that persisted in seeing black people as less than equal or inferior to the dominant population.[6]

The achievement of African Americans in the areas of government, business, and popular culture created a perception that black Americans were now, finally, integrating into mainstream America. But as laudable as these accomplishments were, there still remained some harsh realities that could not be ignored. Poverty among African Americans was disproportionate to their numbers in the society; health issues continued to take a heavy toll no matter the class status; and finally, and most tragically, violence and incarceration among black males was wildly out of control.[7]

Despite the lamentations of black political activists about their situation, it was clear that the political atmosphere of the nation was more intent on placing the onus on African Americans than on considering the effects of racism and class inequality in the structure of American society. And this was only heightened by the fact that as the United States traveled into the twenty-first century, its identity, predicated on a once durable White Anglo-Saxon Protestant work and moral ethic, was rapidly disappearing in the face of an increasing multiracial diasporic diversity.

Even African Americans, however forcibly or voluntarily yoked to the liberal democratic capitalist tradition founded on WASP-ism, faced the reality that Latinos (as of 2004, the largest minority in the nation), Asians, Africans, and peoples of Middle Eastern heritages were reshaping the cultural and racial identity of what it meant to be an American. Historically, all of these groups interacted with African American intellectuals in various ways. But the twenty-first century posed new challenges for black intellectuals as they had to search for ways to renegotiate meanings of identity and racial formation in a nation where the white populace was in decline yet still maintained control of the political economy.[8]

The visibility of black intellectuals and the accomplishments made through the Civil Rights movement may well have opened new vistas for black people in the United States, but it also raised the level of tension that still existed in a culture embedded with racism and white supremacy. These features' ongoing presence could be documented in the violent attacks on African Americans by white supremacist groups; racial profiling by law enforcement agencies that could and did, at times, turn deadly; and an apparent disregard for the black poor whether they suffered in natural disasters such as Hurricane Katrina in 2005 or socioeconomic travesties that led to virulent illness or violence.

Racist suspicions about black capabilities continued to bubble beneath the surface of a United States that many in power, black and white, wanted to project as color-blind. The cruel irony was that the more black American intellectuals became visible, the more their intellect and raison d'être were questioned. Princeton University philosopher, theologian, and activist Cornel West was a prime example. The 1980s and '90s were an active period for what West has called the "insurgent black intellectual." Mainstream intellectual magazines such as the *New Yorker* devoted column space to African American intellectuals such as Hilton Als and the head of Harvard University's W. E. B. Du Bois Institute, Henry "Skip" Louis Gates Jr.[9]

By 1996, Gates had recruited some of the country's best-known African American intellectuals into the Du Bois Institute, Harvard's African American studies department. Operating with nearly a blank check from Harvard's president, Neil Rudenstine, Gates, a notable networker and bridge builder, managed to bring William Julius Wilson, the urban sociologist from the University of Chicago; his good friend the Ghanaian American philosopher Kwame Anthony Appiah from Duke University; former federal judge A. Leon Higginbotham and his wife, historian Evelyn Higginbotham; and Cornel West from Princeton University. This intellectually formidable group joined other black intellectuals already at Harvard, sociologist Orlando Patterson and law professors Randall Kennedy and Charles Ogletree.[10]

As a result, Harvard became the leading center for African American intellectuals in the nation. Over the next ten years, the "Harvard Dream Team" would go about the work that all Harvard academicians do: engage in research designed to have an impact on the policies and destiny of the United States. Gates would bring on board the legal scholar Lani Guinier as the first tenured African American woman in the law school. Additionally, Gates raised $40 million dollars for the department. It appeared that Harvard had not only demonstrated a ringing endorsement of diversity in the academy but also influenced other major PWIs to enhance their black studies programs. Princeton maintained its African American studies program after Cornel West's departure with such distinguished scholars as Nell Irvin Painter and Albert Raboteau. Columbia University gained the activists/scholars Manning Marable and Robin D. G. Kelley, as well as Barbara Jeanne Fields and Winston James. The University of Chicago housed Thomas Holt, a former president of the American Historical Association and scholar of African American and Southern history, and Julie Saville, the Southern historian. Stanford University, since the mid-1980s, was the home of the Martin Luther King Jr. Papers Project, directed by a historian of SNCC, Clayborne Carson.

As these examples demonstrate, the visibility and influence of black thinkers firmly settled into the mainstream American academy. However politically volatile that presence was, there was no denying that the intellectual foundations for elaborating a dynamic cosmopolitan diasporic diversity was under way.[11] That may have been the reason for the intellectual push back that took place after Neil Rudenstine left Harvard in 2001. Rudenstine's successor approached Harvard's presidency very differently. As a former secretary of the treasury under President Bill Clinton, Lawrence Summers was known for his tenaciously aggressive intellectual manner. Like Cornel West, he was no stranger to Harvard; both men were prodigies born a year apart (West was born in 1953 and Summers in 1954). Their academic trajectories rose in the 1980s as West completed his doctorate at Princeton in philosophy and Summers was a student and later professor of economics at Harvard before entering the political realm. Both men, in their own ways, had amassed credible resumes. But they were destined to clash in an era that was steeped in clashes over cultural matters regarding race, diversity, national security against terrorism, and a profound change in how the United States saw itself.[12]

Certainly, West was no stranger to controversy. Born in Tulsa, Oklahoma, but raised in Los Angeles, his parents eked out a living that placed the family in the lower middle class. West early on demonstrated a hunger for intellectual stimulation. That eagerness for attaining knowledge landed him in a coveted spot at Harvard University. There he thrived and soaked up the intellectual atmosphere that the nation's premier university was noted for. Completing his undergraduate studies, West took his doctorate in philosophy at Princeton University studying with the well-known, brilliant, and provocative philosopher Richard Rorty. It was Rorty's analytical take on American pragmatism that gave Cornel West the hook on which to hang the varied threads of his own thinking. Picking and choosing from Karl Marx, John Rawls, John Dewey, and the more liberal theological wing of Protestantism (West was deeply involved in the black church and had taught at Union Theological Seminary) enabled West to propose a progressive "prophetic pragmatism" that could serve as a political tool for change as well as an intellectual articulation for the black Left.[13]

Such intellectual ambitions were soon to be heavily scrutinized. West's recruitment away from Princeton to become a member of Harvard's faculty became the occasion for his work and thought to be critically evaluated. Such a happening should have been no real concern. After all, scholars look forward to and are often gratified when their writings, theories, or philosophies are critically discussed however laudably or contentiously. But instead it was, once again, a demonstration that no matter how visible African American intellectuals now were, even in the twenty-first century, they were not taken seriously. Cornel

West's scholarship was subjected to blistering criticism by the *New Republic*'s chief cultural critic Leon Wieseltier (himself a Harvard graduate). Calling West's thinking "incomprehensible," the article all but called Cornel West an intellectual charlatan.[14]

The article created a firestorm among left and liberal pundits. For those on the left who saw Cornel West as a brilliant intellectual/activist, the *New Republic* piece was a libel. But others, especially Lawrence Summers, the new president of Harvard, were greatly influenced by the article.[15] It was already apparent to the black scholars in Harvard's African American department that Lawrence Summers was cool toward them. William Julius Wilson early on had voiced concerns that Summers did not seem to hold black studies or the black faculty in high regard. When Summers met with the department (having held them off for some time), Wilson's worries were realized. Even worse, Summers clearly evinced an uncertainty as to whether diversity or affirmative action was all that important.[16]

Then Henry Louis Gates received a phone call from Summers, who expressed concern over the size of one of West's classes (over 600 students enrolled in the Introduction to African American Studies course), his contribution to grade inflation, his release of a rap record, and finally his political activities in 2000 (first with presidential contender Bill Bradley, then with Al Sharpton). Summers arranged for a meeting with West and seventeen other professors to discuss his projects. Summers indicated at that meeting that he wanted more serious scholarship from West. West had published a highly successful book of essays in the early 1990s, *Race Matters*.[17]

Certainly, Summers had the right, if not the duty, to inquire into the work of that group of university professors. Although he was considered "extremely smart," however, Summers was also "famously abrasive" in a confrontational manner. This would be his undoing in 2005 when he questioned whether women had the intellectual capacities to do serious work in the natural sciences. Despite numerous apologies afterwards, the faculty voted no confidence twice and Summers eventually resigned. The new president of Harvard University would be not only a person more closely connected to the academy (which Summers had not been) but also Harvard University's first woman president, historian Drew Gilpin Faust.[18]

But before these events unfolded, more consequences emerged from Summers's meeting with West. Summers did not believe that West's activities were of sufficiently rigorous scholarship. Clearly one could make the argument that West had, over the course of the 1990s, become more of a public intellectual (and celebrity). His collaborative work with other black scholars such as bell hooks, the making of a spoken-word record that was received as "rap" music, and various political activities including participation in Louis Farrakhan's Million Man March in 1995 all demonstrated solidarity with a politics of black liberation and his belief in a pragmatic prophetic radical democracy.[19]

Admittedly, Cornel West's thinking was often a jumble of ideas and connections that never quite seemed to add up to anything earth shattering. It was reminiscent of Harold Cruse's more cogent but ultimately failed attempts to theorize and concretize a pluralistic black nationalist ethics and politics. Nonetheless, West's public intellectual activities should not be held against him. He himself admitted to owing a debt to intellectuals of the recent past such as Lionel Trilling and Richard Hofstader. Besides, West's activities, however provocative or questionable in judgment, were nothing compared to the ideas of William Shockley, a physicist who spouted racist theories about gene pools. And were Arthur Jensen's educational studies purportedly demonstrating racial inferiority among African Americans really rigorous scholarship? In both cases academe did little to discredit the work. Shockley and Jensen were not called into their respective university president's or dean of faculty's offices for the close questioning that West received from Lawrence Summers. If anything, the cloak of legitimacy was conferred on this kind of "academic scholarship" with the publication in the 1990s of Richard Herrnstein and Charles Murray's *The Bell Curve*.[20]

The confrontation between Lawrence Summers and Cornel West resulted in attempts by Summers at apologies and appeasement. But West would have none of that. By the time the dust had settled, the celebrated "Harvard Dream Team" had awakened to the sober reality of academic racism. Over the next two years many of the scholars that Skip Gates recruited left the university for what they considered more hospitable climes. Christopher Edly went to California; West went back to Princeton and was joined shortly afterwards by Kwame Anthony Appiah. Even Gates thought about leaving Harvard to go to Princeton but opted for staying and helping rebuild the black studies program.[21]

What this debacle demonstrated was a two-edged sword for African American intellectuals entering the twenty-first century. On one edge was the once again stark realization that black scholars, no matter how visible they had become, were nonetheless marginalized and criticized as spokespersons for "The Race." And yet as Michael Eric Dyson has pointed out, "Black intellectuals turned a deficit into a credit. They were limited to writing or speaking in public about race. As a result, the subject is now viewed the way black intellectuals have longed viewed it, as the central problem of American society, through the eyes of thinkers who have witnessed the bitter triumphs of racism while working feverishly for its defeat."[22]

Though this could be said to be the other edge of the sword for African American intellectuals, there remained the challenge of not only "working feverishly" for the demise of racism but moving to a place where black intellectuals are truly able to use ideas and the life of the mind to provide a vision for what the nation and humanity should strive for. As the multitalented Charles Johnson noted in his essay, "The Role of the Black Intellectual in the Twenty-first Century," "The objective of the *next* century should be, if we are wise, the development of a generation of black scholars capable of speaking with authority and enthusiasm on *any* and *all* subjects that define the human condition."[23] Johnson's statement has a precedent: in 1992, two years before his death, Ralph Ellison, upon receiving the Chicago Public Library Harold Washington Literacy Award, stated, "It isn't a color question anymore—color is just an excuse. People have taken advantage of others because of religion, hairstyle, everything. People have to be brave enough to express themselves and learn from others."[24]

These words, spoken nine years before 9/11/01 and the United States' immersion into an atmosphere of war and obsession with security from terrorism not only provided the foundation for Johnson's 2003 essay but served as a historical bridge on which future generations of African American intellectuals could build. It is a bridge that stretches from the promised hope of a popular cultural front in the 1930s through to a Civil Rights revolution that informed and shaped an interracial coalition committed to equality and freedom for all humanity. That bridge arced and showed hope in the waning days of the first decade of the twenty-first century as the nation's presidential campaign of 2008 brought forth a diverse group of candidates from both political parties. But it was within the Democratic Party that there arose a trajectory that may have a more enduring historical impact on the United States' racial dilemma and sense of its self. In this party there was a white woman, Hillary Rodham Clinton, the former first lady, and Barack Hussein Obama, the African American senator from Illinois (the state where Ellison made that acceptance speech) who were serious contenders for the presidency.

Both captured the interest and support of African American masses. But it was Obama who, within the dictates of a liberal democratic ethos, articulated a message that held the promise of forging a dynamic cosmopolitan diversity that recognized the central importance of the African disapora to the American enterprise. If ever there was a moment for African American intellectuals to truly come into visibility with intellectual authority and enthusiasm, that new day was dawning. But not without first dealing with the ramifications, both intellectual and political, of Obama's emergence.

With the march to the nomination of Barack Obama, African American intellectuals were confronted and challenged with the full implications of diasporic diversity. Not only did they have to grapple with the rapidly shifting meanings of race in a nation still deeply troubled by that issue, but they had to regain the confidence of the black masses and to replenish what little moral capital they had left. That meant finding the means to confront racism and embrace diasporic diversity and the idea of a truly multiracial/multicultural America. It promised to be a tough challenge. Nonetheless, with Obama's ever stronger grip on the nomination, what African American intellectuals had going for them was a living embodiment of what diasporic diversity could look like in twenty-first-century America.

Obama's father, Barack Sr., was an African born and raised in Kenya. He met Obama's mother, Stanley Ann Dunham, while attending school in the United States. She was a young, free-spirited white woman from Kansas. They married and lived in Hawai'i where Barack was born. Later, Barack's father abandoned the family, went to Harvard University, and from there back to Kenya. Though young Barack did not know his father intimately, he would later in life connect with the African side of his family. Meanwhile, his mother divorced Barack Sr. and married Lolo Sotero, from Indonesia. The family moved there, where Barack was schooled in public and private educational institutions. From the beginning, then, Barack Obama experienced a world of diasporic diversity.[25]

Obama's early years saw him grappling with racial formations that grew out of his being a biracial person. In the end, he self-identified as an African American. But that came only after much reading, pondering, and reflection on what race meant in the United States. One of his inspirations was the Civil Rights movement and in particular, SNCC workers in the South attempting to register poor black sharecroppers to vote. As Obama put it, "Such images became a form of prayer for me, bolstering my spirits, channeling my emotions in a way that words never could."[26]

The words were illuminating, for they echoed the founding resolution of the Student Nonviolent Coordinating Committee. The resolution had stated, "We affirm the philosophical or religious idea of non-violence as the foundation of our purpose, the pre-supposition of our faith, and the manner of our action. Non-violence . . . seeks a social order of justice permeated by love. Integration of human endeavor represents the crucial first step towards such a society."[27] Obama certainly took those steps. He read Richard Wright, James Baldwin, and the autobiography of Malcolm X. In his later schooling, he sought out the politically active black students and the tenured white Marxist professors. He soaked up as much knowledge as he could, informing a racial identity that was diverse in his being black, internationally conscious, and an individual.[28]

By the time Obama reached Harvard University law school, his mind was well-equipped and his identity was firmly in place. At Harvard, he began a string of successes that led to the greatest journey of his life. He became the first African American editor of the *Harvard Law Review*. When he obtained his degree in law, Obama returned to Chicago, where he engaged in community organizing on the South Side, helping the residents there register to vote. When he had interned one summer at a law firm, he met Michelle Robinson, herself a Harvard law graduate. They married after Obama worked in a law firm that specialized in civil rights cases and began a teaching stint at the University of Chicago law school. Obama married Robinson deep in the heart of Chicago's black world; a world Obama was very familiar with. He had become a member of Trinity United Church of Christ, which was led by Reverend Jeremiah Wright Sr., an ex-marine who had fought in Korea and later became a devoted disciple of black liberation theology. Reverend Wright presided over the marriage of Michelle and Barack in 1992.[29]

Obama taught three courses at the University of Chicago law school, including an original one on racism and the law. His students noted his method of contextualization and wariness of grand theory. Obama clearly believed in the process of American legal jurisprudence. In this regard, he found himself in the hallowed company of many outstanding African American legalists from Thurgood Marshall to Charles Houston to Randall Kennedy and Lani Guinier.[30]

The Obamas settled in the integrated and progressive Hyde Park neighborhood of Chicago. It was from here that Harold Washington made his historic and successful run to be the first black mayor of the Windy City. Obama split his time between teaching at the University of Chicago law school and doing community organizing. He helped register thousands of voters for the campaign of Carol Mosley Braun, the first African American woman to be elected to the U.S. Senate in 1992.[31]

In 1995, Barack Obama stepped into the political ring and ran for the Illinois State Senate. The entry marked the beginning of not only the Obama style of politics but, in general, of a new style of black politics that emerged in the wake of the post–Civil Rights–integration–affirmative action era. These were young black politicians who understood—indeed, had integrated—into the political system of the nation. In both of the major political parties, this class of new black politicos had learned how to win over white voters and maintain ties to black communities while at the same time managing to mute overt appeals to race. In most cases, it was a successful combination. It certainly worked in Obama's favor.[32]

Obama served in the Illinois State Senate and moved on issues such as ethics reform and insensitive police tactics in the black community. Still, nothing spectacular stood out from his term. Obama tried to run for Congress against the well-known black politician and former Black Panther member Bobby Rush and was soundly beaten. After taking stock of the situation, Barack Obama made a move that demonstrated a willingness to take risks but also displayed a developing maturity and rising confidence. Post-9/11 America was gripped with fear and anxiety over terrorist attacks that many thought could never happen let alone cause such devastation. In 2002, as war clouds gathered, Barack Obama considered making a speech decrying the need to rush into war. He did not oppose all wars but called going to war in Iraq "dumb." The speech, which would be a key element in his run for the presidency, was carefully balanced but clearly showed that he was against an invasion of Iraq.[33]

Then, a U.S. Senate seat opened up in 2004 and Obama, carefully this time, entered the race. His two major opponents would later drop out. Obama, having been selected to give the keynote address at the Democratic National Convention in Boston, ignited the crowd and presaged what might occur. That keynote address was most important in its demonstration of what Obama believed the twenty-first-century

American identity would look like. It contained passages that spoke not just to a few constituencies but rather knitted them into a whole fabric that was at once diverse and yet singular. An example passage, worth a lengthy quote, could only have been written by a skilled African American intellectual for the twenty-first century:

> Now even as we speak, there are those who are preparing to divide us, the spin masters and negative ad peddlers who embrace the politics of anything goes. Well I say to them, tonight, there is not a liberal America and a conservative America—there is the United States of America. There is not a Black America and White America, and Latino America and Asian America—there is the United States of America.
>
> The pundits like to slice and dice our country into Red States and Blue States, Red States for Republicans, Blue States for Democrats. But, I've got news for them. We worship an awesome God in the Blue States, and we don't like federal agents poking around our libraries in the Red States. We coach Little League in the Blue States, and yes, we've got some gay friends in the Red States. There are patriots who opposed the war in Iraq, and there are patriots who supported the war in Iraq.
>
> We are one people, all of us pledging allegiance to the Stars and Stripes, all of us defending the United States of America.[34]

The cadence in the delivery, the smooth delineation of who and what the United States was, showed off not only Obama's oratorical skills but also his refashioning of a liberal democratic nationalist vision that at once stood apart from the divisive and (and exclusive) nature of the political conservative reign of the last generation and embraced an inclusive society that held key elements of diasporic diversity.

Obama won the U.S. Senate seat from Illinois in 2004 with 70 percent of the vote. Dutifully, the junior senator went to work for his state and for the country. Though there was no doubt that his stands were solidly liberal, he was not of the knee-jerk variety; indeed some progressives were uncomfortable that Obama did not take a harsher stance on the Iraq war from his seat on the Foreign Relations Committee. But Obama was uncomfortable with the Washington milieu; he missed his wife and daughters, Malia and Sasha. He determinedly commuted home to Chicago every weekend to be with them. While in Washington, he tended to business and worked out in a Chinatown athletic club instead of the more comfortable Senate gym. As it turned out, Obama was the Democratic Party's most sought after fund-raiser and campaigner. Younger than most of his Senate colleagues, Obama demonstrated an ability to raise millions of dollars especially through the use of the Internet. Obama, in more ways than one, showed a growing shift and change in the American sociopolitical landscape.[35]

That landscape, overshadowed for so long by contentious culture wars over gay rights, abortion, public displays of Christian icons like the Ten Commandments, and creationism, to name but a few hot-spots, also saw shifts in the way race mattered and shaped peoples, especially young people's consciousness. Here Barack Obama was a prime example of what that change meant. Racial identification in the early-twenty-first-century United States continued to be angst-ridden especially in the baby-boomer black middle class who came of age in the Civil Rights era and survived that tumultuous period. Pride in blackness yet an earnest desire to be fully accepted as American citizens continued to be a stressful dilemma. What exacerbated that warring consciousness was the need to find not only balance but an authentication for what blackness really meant. It was here that matters became troubling.

After years (and in the historical long view it could be said to be continuous) of battling a pervasive belief on the part of whites that black behavior constituted a social pathology, that battle continued as young people, black and white, embraced hip-hop as a signature of racial authenticity. Yet the hip-hop culture seemed to reinforce the very ideas that middle-class blacks were fighting against. It did not help matters that movies and television, in addition to the music, presented a world where blackness meant overcoming the mean streets (with violence), going for the "bling" (with no real attention to the moral implications or consequences of such endeavors), and capturing as many women as possible (often objectified as playthings that were quickly discarded). Within the larger cultural context of the older generation, this evolution of hip-hop was a reflection of the unfettered, anything goes, market rules mentality fostered since the 1980s.

And yet intellectuals, black and white, Left and Right continued to offer the same analyses and prescriptions for this state of affairs. Conservatives, from the 1980s into the first decade of the twenty-first century, pointed to the social behaviors that seeped out of the inner cities and poisoned the general social fabric. Liberals and the Left saw racism in old and new forms, whether institutional or environmental, as creating the conditions that cut off a disproportionate number of black Americans (and other minorities) from opportunities for safe, healthy, and successful lives.

Thus it was no accident that as Barack Obama barnstormed around the county campaigning on the need for the United States to change, a key ingredient in his vision was one of inclusion and a transparency that would ensure Americans would be seen nationally and internationally as a multiracial, diasporic, diverse land. Shrewdly, Obama did not always specifically talk about race, and in that regard his domestic policy visions hewed closely to black urban sociologist William Julius Wilson's synthetic analyses that encompassed elements of the Left's and Right's analyses.

Wilson, formerly of the University of Chicago sociology department and presently at the Du Bois Institute in Harvard, was clearly a legatee of those young "black Turks" of the 1930s who saw economic and class issues as being as important if not more important than race. Wilson had burst on the intellectual scene in the late 1970s with a first book that touted the declining significance of race due to the successes of the Civil Rights movement and its role in creating the largest ever black middle class. The movement of that newly enlarged black middle class out of the inner cities and into the suburbs left behind a population that, due to shifting economic circumstances ranging from a decline in manufacturing to the outsourcing of jobs overseas, was mired in low-wage jobs or no meaningful employment at all. Crime, drug use, and dangerous health conditions filled the vacuum and created a miserable existence of poverty. For Wilson, a new social vision had to be undertaken.[36]

Wilson's prescriptions for the black poverty in the nation's inner cities, reminiscent of the 1930s debates regarding race, class, and an economy in crisis, found resonance in Obama's vision for change. As a presidential contender, Obama ran on those issues that in 2007–2008 were uppermost in Americans minds: the war in Iraq, health care, and, looming ever so large, an economy entering a recession. Race, however much it bubbled beneath the political seas, did not appear to be a major concern. Not, that is, until the matter of racial identity was raised.

In January 2007, at the online political and cultural commentary site Salon.com, Debra J. Dickerson, an independent African American commentator, raised the issue that, quite frankly, was talked about in black communities across the country. Dickerson hesitated to write about the issue—"For me it was a trick question in a game I refused to play"—but she nonetheless put forth a provocative statement on racial identity when linked to the question of whether the nation was ready for a black man or a white woman (Hillary Rodham Clinton, a senator from New York) to be president. "Since the issue," Dickerson wrote, "was always framed as a battle between gender and race (read nonwhiteness—the question is moot when all the players are white), I didn't have the heart (or the stomach) to point out the obvious: Obama isn't black."[37]

But this definition of blackness proved problematic. "'Black' in our political and social reality, means those descended from West African slaves," Dickerson asserted. "Voluntary immigrants of African descent (even those descended from West Indian slaves) are just that, voluntary immigrants of African descent with markedly different outlooks on the role of race in their lives and politics." In one fell swoop, Dickerson discounted the whole role, meaning, or efficacy of diasporic diversity. To go by her limited definition of blackness, outstanding black intellectuals such as Alexander Crummell (African), W. E. B. Du Bois (New Englander and Afro-Caribbean), and James Weldon Johnson (Afro-Caribbean and fluent in Latino cultures) were not really black. Dickerson wrote that "at minimum, it can't be assumed that a Nigerian cabdriver and a third-generation Harlemite have more in common than the fact a cop won't bother to make the distinction. They're both 'black' as a matter of skin color and DNA, but only the Harlemite, for better or worse, is politically and culturally black, as we use the term."[38]

In addition, it had to be asked, what did this say about African Americans from the West Coast or the Midwest? Are only urban blacks who have some ties to slavery the only "true" blacks? It appeared that behind Dickerson's refusal to see Barack Obama as "black" was a criticism that white Americans "are engaged in a paroxysm of self congratulation." For Dickerson, whites were "not embracing a black man, a descendant of slaves. You're *replacing* the black man with an immigrant of recent African descent of whom you can approve without feeling either guilty or frightened."[39]

Dickerson believed that a "white woman will be the Democratic nominee for president before a black descendant of American slaves." Of course calling into question Barack Obama's racial lineage was a tricky matter on several levels. It could be pointed out there are scores of well-known African Americans who are biracial: Booker T. Washington, Mary Church Terrell, Frederick Douglass, to name but a few examples. On another level, historically, can those black abolitionists of the North who may have had no ties to slavery be discounted as "black"? And how were Africans brought to the United States from the Caribbean to places such as South Carolina or Georgia to be regarded? The limits of Dickerson's definition of who was or is black, in the end, could not sustain intellectual clarity or credibility. One sharp response came in February 2007 when Julius Lester stated on his blog, *A Commonplace Book,* "All of this would be funny if it were not so utterly ridiculous. Blacks who submit other blacks to a racial litmus test are no different than whites who submit blacks to a racial litmus test. There is an almost total void of black leadership nationally because what too many blacks are seeking is someone who will make them feel good about being black, not someone who has creative ideas about how to address the problems not only faced by blacks but by America."[40] Lester approached the matter no less candidly but more honestly than Dickerson when he observed, after Obama's election, "Like most blacks, I didn't think a black man had a chance of being elected president, especially a black man with a foreign name. To be honest, I think that the initial response to Obama's chances came not only from our perception of a racist white America. That initial response also came from residual feelings of black inferiority."[41]

The persistent search for a positive and uplifting racial identity has driven African American intellectuals to develop various methods or, to use a more apt term suggested by Charles Johnson, "narratives," that often placed black Americans as victims of a pernicious white racism grounded in slavery. Clearly, however, that narrative became all encompassing once racism was seen as not only a racial binary (black versus white) but also as institutionalized and systemic to the point that the legacy of slavery became almost an afterthought.[42] How peculiar then it was that in a post–Civil Rights era when segregation's stifling racial barriers were demolished and affirmative action through education created a large (and for the most part successful) black intellectual and professional middle class, that now the slave experience became *the* criterion for being black—especially that this occurred at a moment when an African American appeared who represented the best of what diasporic diversity embodied and had a serious chance of being elected president of the United States.

The fear of a new "narrative" was strong among the black elite; black victimization had served many purposes. Gerald Early commented, "The presidential campaign of Barack Obama has raised the question of what happens to the black American meta-narrative of heroic or noble victimization if he wins." That victimization narrative presented itself provocatively in the remarks of Barack Obama's pastor at Trinity United Church of Christ in Chicago, the Reverend Jeremiah Wright.[43]

Clips of Reverend Wright's emotional, passion-filled sermons attacking American racism flooded the Internet, providing Republicans and conservatives with ammunition to designate Obama as being racially divisive. Matters heated up when Reverend Wright praised Louis Farrakhan's views (one of the more extreme black victimization narratives) as bringing "a perspective that is helpful and honest . . . one of the most important voices in the 20th and 21st centur[ies]." Obama, at first, distanced himself from Wright, stating that his claims were a "bunch of rants that aren't grounded in truth."[44] But as the matter threatened to overshadow the campaign by raising perennial racial divisions and perceptions, Barack Obama turned the situation into an educative moment to clear the air on race. In Philadelphia on March 18, 2008, Obama gave a speech that many among his campaign staff felt he should avoid: a speech that tackled not just Reverend Wright's remarks but the whole issue of race in American society.

Obama was clear when he repeated, "I have already condemned, in unequivocal terms, the statements of Reverend Wright that caused such controversy." And yet Obama made it equally clear how interwoven the fabric of the nation was when it came to race: "I can no more disown him [Wright] than I can disown the black community. I can no more disown him than I can my white grandmother." For Obama recognized how deeply the blood ties of black and white ran in American society and the effects that racial division can have on all Americans. He noted that his grandmother was a woman who raised him, sacrificed for him, and who "loves me as much as she loves anything in this world." But Obama's grandmother also harbored a fear of "black men who passed by her on the street" and "on more than one occasion has uttered racial or ethnic stereotypes that made me cringe."[45]

But despite these tragic flaws in Wright and his grandmother, they were part of Obama and they were America, "this country I love." It was from here that Obama laid the framework for what could become a new way of thinking, talking, even creating a new narrative about race. Stating bluntly that "race is an issue that I believe this nation cannot afford to ignore right now," he asserted, "In the white community, the path to a more perfect union means acknowledging that what ails the African American community does not just exist in the minds of black people; that the legacy of discrimination, and current incidents of discrimination, while less overt than in the past, are real and must be addressed." Obama saw this happening not "just with words but with deeds." Civil rights laws must be enforced, fairness in the justice system must be ensured, and opportunities for generations to come must be provided. And these must be done through Americans realizing that "investing in the health, welfare, and education of black, brown, and white children will ultimately help all of America prosper."

For African Americans, Obama was equally forthright stating that the path to a more perfect union "means embracing the burdens of our past without becoming the victims of our past." While African Americans must continue to insist on full justice in all aspects of the nation's life, they must also bind "our particular grievances . . . to the larger aspirations of all Americans."[46] For Obama, this was where the new narrative begins: with a nation moving toward a more perfect union through the creation of a new narrative that recognized race but also sought to move past it. This speech elevated the Obama campaign and most probably won over most white and black Americans, including most of the nation's intellectuals.[47]

On November 4, 2008, Barack H. Obama was elected forty-fourth president of the United States. He was the first black man in U.S. history to be elected. The vote was unquestionably in the majority. On January 20, 2009, Barack Obama was sworn in as millions crowded Washington, D.C., and millions more watched on television or the Internet.

African American intellectuals were ecstatic about the historic event. Orlando Patterson, the black sociologist and public intellectual, stated in a *New York Times* op-ed that "Barack Obama's victory marks the end of another magnificent chapter in America's experience with democracy." Henry Louis Gates Jr., warning that all of the problems of black children, or even black Americans, would not suddenly disappear, nonetheless enthusiastically proclaimed that "without question . . . the election of Obama as President of the United States means that 'the Ultimate Color Line' . . . has, at long last, been crossed. It has been crossed by our very first postmodern race man, a man who embraces his African cultural and genetic heritage so securely that he can transcend it." Alice Walker poetically observed that "we knew through all generations that you were with us, in us, the best of the spirit of Africa and of Americas." But perhaps Julius Lester stated it best when he recalled his feelings on the day after the inauguration: "As I live with the emotional memory of those millions of people on the mall in Washington, joy pouring from their bodies as if it were a radiant light, I realized that the revolution we fought for in the '60s is finally over, and we won."[48]

What then is to be done? African American intellectuals in the twenty-first century can take their cue from an Obama presidency and the words that he spoke in Philadelphia during his race for the nomination. They can become a "transformative black intelligentsia." That means that these black intellectuals would seek a new narrative that clearly remembered the past as it calls for civil rights and social justice for blacks (especially the poor). It would mean a continued movement to eradicate racism and discrimination and a move to create a truly diverse and equal society. At the same time, any thought that there will be a unification in the voices of those intellectuals must be questioned. Black conservatives such as Thomas Sowell, John McWhorter, or Shelby Steele, to name a few, may well address and decry discrimination based on race. But they also move away from embracing a transformative black intelligentsia in favor of a conservative color-blind society. Black liberal and leftist intellectuals such as Henry Louis Gates Jr., Cornel West, Adolph L. Reed Jr., bell hooks, Michael Eric Dyson, and Alice Walker, again to name but a few, may also broaden their ideas about racial formations and identity in favor of a more cosmopolitan or multicultural viewpoint.[49]

In the end, the Du Boisian notion of transformative intellectuals emanating out of the black middle class has over time come into being and now is faced with new and difficult but exciting challenges regarding racial identity in the United States in an age when the first black American has been elected president. It is truly the beginning of a new chapter in an integrated American history.

NOTES

BIBLIOGRAPHY

INDEX

NOTES

Introduction: What Is an African American Intellectual?

1. See Banks, *Black Intellectuals*; Joy James, *Transcending the Talented Tenth*; Cruse, *The Crisis of the Negro Intellectual*; C. West, "The Dilemma of the Black Intellectual."

2. See Kilson, "Styles of Black Intellectuals"; C. West, "The Dilemma of the Black Intellectual"; Posner, *Public Intellectuals*.

3. Frazier, *Black Bourgeoisie*; Cox, *Caste, Class, and Race*; Holt, *The Problem of Race in the Twenty-first Century*; Banner-Haley, *The Fruits of Integration*.

4. Holt, *The Problem of Race in the Twenty-first Century*, 18.

5. Quoted in Posner, *Public Intellectuals*, 31.

6. Moses, "Culture, Civilization, and the Decline of the West"; for a full fleshing out of these matters, see Lewis, *W. E. B. Du Bois: Biography of a Race* and *W. E. B. Du Bois: The Fight for Equality and the American Century*.

7. Moses, "Culture, Civilization, and the Decline of the West," 244; Lewis, *W. E. B. Du Bois: The Fight for Equality and the American Century*, chapters 8–9.

8. Robert Hemenway, *Zora Neale Hurston*; see also Boyd, *Wrapped in Rainbows*.

9. Richard Wright's chief biographer is Michel Fabre. See his *The Unfinished Quest of Richard Wright*. A more recent biography that covers the writings of *Uncle Tom's Children* and *Native Son* nicely is Rowley, *Richard Wright*.

10. On Ellison's background, see Lawrence Jackson, *Ralph Ellison*, chapters 1–2; Rampersad, *Ralph Ellison*, chapter 1. For Hurston see Hurston, *Dust Tracks on a Road*, 1–4, and Boyd, *Wrapped in Rainbows*, chapters 1–2. On Wright, see Fabre, *Unfinished Quest*, chapters 1–3, and Rowley, *Richard Wright*, chapters 1–3. But see also Wright, *Black Boy* and *American Hunger*.

11. Lester, introduction to Killian, *Black and White Reflections of a White Southern Sociologist*, xi.

12. Dyson, *Mike on Mike* and *Debating Race*; Kelley, *Freedom Dreams*; Morrison, *Playing in the Dark*; McGruder, *The Boondocks* and *A Right to Be Hostile*.

13. McGruder, *All the Rage*; see also *The Boondocks: The Complete First Season*, DVD.

14. Sowell, *A Man of Letters* and *A Personal Odyssey*; Steele, *The Content of Our Character* and *White Guilt*; McWhorter, *Losing the Race* and *Winning the Race*.

15. McWhorter, *Authentically Black*.

1. The Emergence of the Black Public Intellectual: Race, Class, and the Struggle against Racism

1. On the Depression in Philadelphia, see Banner-Haley, *To Do Good and to Do Well*. An excellent general overview can be found in Sitkoff, *A New Deal for Blacks*, chapters 1–2.

2. There are of course many works that address the presence of Jim Crow segregation in the South. A recent thoroughly researched and poignantly rendered addition to that body of work is Litwack, *Trouble in Mind*. For the North, see Sacks, *Before Harlem*. The personal account of Richard Wright's experiences with segregation can be found in *Black Boy*. Ralph Ellison's mishap and run-in with the brutality of segregation is detailed in Lawrence Jackson, *Ralph Ellison*, chapter 4, and Rampersad, *Ralph Ellison*, chapter 2.

3. The two standard treatments of the New Negro movement, more popularly known as the Harlem Renaissance, are Huggins, *Harlem Renaissance,* and Lewis, *When Harlem Was in Vogue*. On deracialized discourse, see Posnock, *Color and Culture*, chapter 3.

4. Goggin, *Carter G. Woodson,* remains the best biography of Woodson. But see also Meghan Keita, *Race and the Writing of History*, chapter 4.

5. See, of course, Du Bois, *The Souls of Black Folk*; Lewis, *W. E. B. Du Bois: Biography of a Race,* chapter 11, offers a thorough and illuminating discussion of this work. Excellent examples of how Du Bois's double consciousness formulation has been examined by leading African American intellectuals can be found in Early, ed., *Lure and Loathing*. See also the insightful essay by Watts, "The Souls of Black Folk and Afro-American Intellectual Life," in Marable et al., *The Souls of W. E. B. Du Bois*.

6. Lewis, *Du Bois*; Holt, "W. E. B. Du Bois's Archeology of Race," in *W. E. B. Du Bois: Race and the City: The Philadelphia Negro and Its Legacy*, 61–76.

7. There are several fine recent books that address this subject: Scott, *Contempt and Pity*; Singh, *Black Is a Country*; Francille Wilson, *The Segregated Scholars*; and Holloway, *Confronting the Veil*.

8. This overview of the Great Depression is greatly indebted to David Kennedy's powerful work *Freedom from Fear,* prologue and chapters 1–3; Holloway, *Confronting the Veil*, introduction; and Francille Wilson, *The Segregated Scholars*, introduction.

9. Holloway, *Confronting the Veil*, 2.

10. This overview owes much to Lewis, *W. E. B. Du Bois: The Fight for Equality and the American Century,* chapter 9.

11. Lewis, *W. E. B. Du Bois: The Fight for Equality and the American Century*; but see also Holt, "The Political Uses of Alienation."

12. Young, *Black Writers of the Thirties*, chapters 2–3; Lewis, *W. E. B. Du Bois: The Fight for Equality and the American Century,* chapter 9; Holloway, *Confronting the Veil*, chapter 4. It should be noted that while Holloway covers much of the same ground as Young, Young's volume remains a standard treatment. Holloway focuses on the emerging black intelligentsia in this period, which would influence black intellectuals for most of the remaining century.

13. Lewis, *W. E. B. Du Bois: The Fight for Equality and the American Century*, 260–61.

14. On these matters see Maxwell, *New Negro, Old Left*; Denning, *The Cultural Front*; and Cedric Robinson, *Black Marxism*, 218–40.

15. Posnock, *Color and Culture*, chapters 1–3; Rampersad, *Langston Hughes*; James Johnson, *Black Manhattan*. Here and the following discussion of the Harlem Renaissance are drawn from a close reading of Huggins, *Harlem Renaissance,* and Lewis, *When Harlem Was in Vogue*.

16. Tracy, *A Historical Guide to Langston Hughes*, introduction, 9, 11, 13; Smethurst, "The Adventures of a Social Poet."

17. Smethurst, "The Adventures of a Social Poet," 153.

18. Ibid., 146–52; Rowley, *Richard Wright*, is very good at providing background to Wright's early years. The standard treatment of course is Fabre, *The Unfinished Quest of Richard Wright*.

19. Rowley, *Richard Wright*, chapters 5–6.

20. Rowley, *Richard Wright*, looks at Wright's reactions; Hughes's reactions can be found in Rampersad, *The Life of Langston Hughes*. Ralph Ellison's reactions, though quiet, would nevertheless have a significant impact on his political stance; see Rampersad, *Ralph Ellison*, chapter 5. On Joe Louis, see Margolick, *Beyond Glory*.

21. James Johnson, *Along This Way*, 595.

22. Ibid., 595. See also Du Bois, "The Negro and Communism."

23. Young, *Black Writers of the Thirties*, chapter 1; Holloway, *Confronting the Veil*; Rampersad, *Ralph Ellison*, chapter 5; Rowley, *Richard Wright*, chapters 5 and 6; for Margaret Walker's take on these matters, see Walker, *Richard Wright*, especially part 3.

24. Lewis, *W. E. B. Du Bois: A Reader*, 591.

25. Lewis, *Du Bois: The Fight for Equality*, 260–61; Cedric Robinson, *Black Marxism*, 218–40. Winston James, *Holding Aloft the Banner of Ethiopia*, chapters 4 and 5.

26. Holloway, *Confronting the Veil*, chapter 3. But see also Platt, *E. Franklin Frazier Reconsidered*.

27. Frazier, "Le Bourgeoisie Noir," 205, 204.

28. Frazier, *Black Bourgeoisie*; Holloway, *Confronting the Veil*, chapter 1, is a splendid description and analysis of Howard University and its development as a breeding ground for African American intellectuals.

29. Holloway, *Confronting the Veil*, chapter 3, 129; Scott, *Contempt and Pity*, chapter 3; and Frazier, "Le Bourgeoisie Noir," 201.

30. Frazier, "Le Bourgeoisie Noir," 203. Emphasis is in the original text.

31. Platt, *Frazier Remembered*, chapter 2; Holloway, *Confronting the Veil*, 150; Frazier, "Le Bourgeoisie Noir," 202.

32. Banner-Haley, *The Fruits of Integration*, 30; Holloway, *Confronting the Veil*, 196.

33. Frazier, "Le Bourgeoisie Noir," 206; Vernon Williams, *Re-Thinking Race*, 7–10.

34. Vernon Williams, *Re-Thinking Race*, chapters 1 and 2; Meghan Keita, *Race and the Writing of History*.

35. Vernon Williams, *Re-Thinking Race*, chapter 1; the critique of Boas in recent years from the Right is best exemplified in D'Sousa, *The End of Racism*, 144–61.

36. Vernon Williams, *Re-Thinking Race*, chapter 1.

37. Trotter, "From a Raw Deal to a New Deal: 1929–1945," 145. On Madison Grant, see Guerl, *The Color of Race in America*, 27–51.

38. See, for example, Herskovits, *The Myth of the Negro Past*. Hurston recounts her training under Boas in *Dust Tracks on a Road*. Cox, *Caste, Class, and Race*.

39. This debate is rendered in Holloway, *Confronting the Veil*, chapter 3.

40. Holloway, *Confronting the Veil*, chapter 3. But see also Frazier, *The Negro Family in the United States*.

41. Holloway, *Confronting the Veil*, 129.

42. Scott, *Contempt and Pity*, chapter 6, 104–8, is very perceptive on liberals' use of the damaged black psyches and Frazier's embrace of it.

43. Hurston, *Dust Tracks on a Road*. For some examples of how Hurston conducted her fieldwork, see some of her letters to Franz Boas and Melville Herskovits in Kaplan, *Zora Neale Hurston: A Life in Letters*, 185–87.

44. *Dust Tracks on a Road* has this chapter. See Alice Walker, "Looking for Zora."

45. As this study was being written, I benefited greatly from reading what most likely are the first full biography of Oliver C. Cox and an extended analysis of his work. See McAuley, *The Mind of Oliver C. Cox*.

46. See Holloway, *Confronting the Veil*, for the shifts on Harris, Frazier, and Bunche's political stances; Scott, *Contempt and Pity*, chapter 6; Frazier, *Black Bourgeoisie*; Dagbovie, *The Early Black History Movement, Carter G. Woodson, and Lorenzo Johnston Greene*; and Janken, *Rayford W. Logan and the Dilemma of the African American Intellectual*.

47. Lewis, *W. E. B. Du Bois*, vol. 1 and vol. 2, charts these changes in Du Bois; McAuley also assesses Cox's importance as a thinker, *The Mind of Oliver C. Cox*.

48. Lewis, *Du Bois*, vol. 2.

49. On Cox's travails, see McAuley, *The Mind of Oliver C. Cox*, chapter 6. For Ellison, see Rampersad, *Ralph Ellison*, chapters 7–10.

2. Black Intellectuals and the Quest for Legitimacy: Civil Rights, Black Power, and the Expenditure of Moral Capital

1. The literature on the rise of Nazism is vast. Two of the most recent works on Hitler that are excellent histories are Kershaw, *Hitler, 1889–1936; I, Hubris* and *Hitler, 1936–1945: II, Nemesis*. On the rise of Nazism in general and its ideology, see Evans, *The Coming of the Third Reich* and *The Third Reich in Power*. The "double V" slogan was coined in the *Pittsburgh Courier* by editor Robert L. Vann. See Buni, *Robert L. Vann of the Pittsburgh Courier*. On the eugenics movement, see Edwin Black, *War against the Weak*.

2. See Lewis, *W. E. B. Du Bois: The Fight for Equality and the American Century, 1919–1963*, chapter 11; Horne, *Race War: White Supremacy and the Japanese Attack on the British Empire*; and Kearney, *African American Views of the Japanese: Solidarity or Sedition*, chapters 1 and 4.

3. Kearney, *African American Views*, chapter 6; Lewis, *Du Bois*, 2: 461–63, gives a good treatment of Du Bois's apologetics for Japan. For how the Japanese viewed the racial milieu, see Horne, *Race War!* chapter 9.

4. Lewis, *Du Bois*, 2: 390–93, for Hikida; Horne, *Race War!* 57–58; Kearney, *African American Views*, chapters 3–5 on Japanese activities in America's black communities.

5. Kearney, *African American Views*, chapters 3–5; Horne, *Race War!* 56.

6. Kearney, *African American Views*, 85–86; Horne, *Race War!* 56.

7. For an overview of the Popular Front, see Smethurst, *The Black Arts Movement*, chapter 1.

8. Smethurst, *The Black Arts Movement*, chapter 1; Keita, *Race and the Writing of American History: Riddling the Sphinx*, chapter 3.

9. Horne, *Race War!* 51–52. On Langston Hughes's experience with Japan, see Rampersad, *The Life of Langston Hughes: I, Too, Sing America*, 272–74.

10. Kearney, *African American Views*, 85–86; Horne, *Race War!* 56; Lewis, *Du Bois*, 2: 390–93.

11. Smethurst, *The Black Arts Movement*, chapter 1. On Wright see Rowley, *Richard Wright: The Life and Times*, chapter 10 and 252–53.

12. Rampersad, *Ralph Ellison: A Biography*, 167–68; Rampersad, *The Life of Langston Hughes: I, Too, Sing America*, 272–74. See also Lawrence Jackson, *Ralph Ellison*, chapter 10.

13. Rowley, *Richard Wright*, 271–74.

14. Ottley, "Seething with Resentment," 8–9.

15. "Call to America," in *Reporting Civil Rights*, 1–4.

16. Pauli Murray, "A Blueprint for First Class Citizenship," in *Reporting Civil Rights*, 62–67; the quote is from page 67. For more insight into Murray's courageous career in civil rights activism and thought, see Gilmore, *Defying Dixie: The Radical Roots of Civil Rights, 1919–1950*.

17. Myrdal, *An American Dilemma: The Negro Problem and Modern Democracy*. For in-depth coverage of the creation of this study, see Walter A. Jackson, *Gunnar Myrdal and America's Conscience*.

18. See Lewis, *The Fight for Racial Equality*, 448–53, which gives excellent coverage of Du Bois being passed over as head of a study of African Americans. See Drake and Cayton, *Black Metropolis*; for E. Franklin Frazier's studies of the Harlem riot and the black family, see the coverage in Platt, *E. Franklin Frazier Reconsidered*, part 2.

19. Singh, *Black Is a Country*, 127–28.

20. Ibid.; chapter 4 is suggestive on this point, which I take to be my own view.

21. Holloway, *Confronting the Veil*, 160.

22. Singh, *Black Is a Country*, 7; but see also Borstelmann, *The Cold War and the Color Line*, and Dudziak, *Cold War Civil Rights*.

23. McAuley, *The Mind of Oliver Cox*, 39–41, discusses Cox's critique of Frazier. See also Walter Jackson, *Gunnar Myrdal*, 258.

24. McAuley, *The Mind of Oliver Cox*, 39–41.

25. Rampersad, *Ralph Ellison*, 181–82.

26. See Ellison, "*An American Dilemma*: A Review," 328–40.

27. Ibid. On the conservative appropriation of Ellison, see Greg Robinson, "Ralph Ellison, Albert Murray, Stanley Crouch, and Modern Black Conservatism," 151–67.

28. Watts, *Heroism and the Black Intellectual*. My own thoughts on Ellison can be found in "Ralph Ellison and the Invisibility of the Black Intellectual."

29. Banner-Haley, "Ralph Ellison and the Invisibility of the Black Intellectual."

30. Rampersad, *Ralph Ellison*, chapters 5–6; Banner-Haley, "Ralph Ellison and the Invisibility of the Black Intellectual," 160–67.

31. Lawrence Jackson, *Ralph Ellison*, chapters 16–18; Rampersad, *Ralph Ellison*, chapters 13–20, are excellent on Ellison's rise in American letters and intellectual circles.

32. Joseph, *Waiting 'til the Midnight Hour*, is an insightful recounting of the era.

33. Lawrence Jackson, *Ralph Ellison*, chapters 16–18; Rampersad, *Ralph Ellison*, chapters 13–20; Joseph, *Waiting 'til the Midnight Hour*.

34. McPherson, "Indivisible Man," 355–95.

35. Some would say that black neoconservative intellectuals such as Shelby Steele or John McWhorter are catering to white intellectuals. But one must be careful here,

for their thinking does have roots in a black intellectual tradition that could rightly lead to a conservatism that pushes for accommodation and genteel race relations. For an excellent discussion of this, see Michael Rudolph West, *The Education of Booker T. Washington.*

36. Ellison, *Juneteenth*. See also the illuminating insights in Warren, *So Black and Blue.*

37. McPherson, "Indivisible Man," 359.

38. Said, *Representations of the Intellectual*, 10–11.

39. See Banner-Haley, *To Do Good and to Do Well,* chapter 1.

40. There are many volumes on black education in this period and the work of the teachers who helped educate the newly freed African American populace. See, for example, Butchart, *Northern Schools, Southern Blacks, and Reconstruction*; James D. Anderson, *The Education of Blacks in the South, 1860–1935*; Jones, *Soldiers of Light and Love.*

41. Gaines, *Uplifting the Race,* 129.

42. For a sampling of these women's thoughts, see the following: Hine et al., eds., *"We Specialize in the Wholly Impossible,"* and Guy-Sheftall, ed., *Words of Fire: An Anthology of African-American Feminist Thought.*

43. For an excellent analysis of the black women's movement in the early part of this century, see Moses, *The Golden Age of Black Nationalism, 1850–1925.*

44. On the activities of African American intellectuals in the thirties, see Kirby, *Black Americans in the Roosevelt Era*; Egerton, *Speak Now against the Day*; Sullivan, *Days of Hope: Race and Democracy in the New Deal Era.*

45. On the impact of black writers in the intellectual forum, see Young's *Black Writers of the Thirties.* An excellent biography of Carter G. Woodson is Goggin's *Carter G. Woodson: A Life in Black History.* But also see Keita, *Race and the Writing of History,* chapter 4; Keita's observations are cogent and insightful.

46. Egerton, *Speak Now against the Day,* chapter 6, 284–85.

47. See Kirby, *Black Americans in the Roosevelt Era,* chapter 2; and Sitkoff, *A New Deal for Blacks,* chapters 8 and 9.

48. Du Bois, "Separation and Self-Respect," 559.

49. Thus Lewis in his edited collection of Du Bois's writings states, "Integration and class solidarity were strategic agendas rather than sacrosanct ideals that Du Bois was willing to subordinate to the categorical imperative of racial integrity and solidarity." Furthermore, Lewis states that Du Bois's defense was that "he was merely proposing a pragmatic response to the racial segregation that was an ineradicable fact of national life, but one that would ultimately yield before the power of separate ethnic and economic groups finally acting in democratic concert" (*Du Bois: A Reader,* 553). But Holt suggests, "The separate economy was merely a contingent, intermediate step to husband the strength of the black community for that larger struggle—the struggle to do away with *all* economic privilege and oppression. For Du Bois the ultimate goal was always justice for all people. In his vision, blacks should use their unique resources to light the way for the rest of the world" ("The Political Uses of Alienation," 319). Holt's assertions imply an amassing and usage of moral capital, and therefore joins the debates of the controversy in Lewis, *W. E. B. Du Bois: Equality and the American Century,* chapter 9.

50. O'Reilly, *Nixon's Piano,* chapter 3, 110.

51. On these matters, see Carson, *In Struggle*; Lester, *All Is Well*; and Branch, *Parting the Waters*. See also Hagan, *Many Minds, One Heart*.

52. Carmichael and Hamilton, *Black Power*; Malcolm X with Alex Haley, *The Autobiography of Malcolm X*; Cleaver, *Soul on Ice*; Fanon, *The Wretched of the Earth*. It is unclear whether most militants thoroughly read this work, as Fanon was not a separatist. What is clear is that his ideas about cathartic violence by the oppressed resonated with the anger that many of the young black militants were feeling. See also Joseph, *Waiting 'til the Midnight Hour*, for an insightful analysis of this movement.

53. I will only give a few examples here as a book could be composed of the work that this generation of black intellectuals has produced. In the area of fiction, see the work of Ralph Ellison, *Invisible Man*, as well as his nonfiction essays in Callahan, ed., *The Collected Essays of Ralph Ellison*. Julius Lester also fits in both fiction and nonfiction commentary. See Lester's *Do Lord Remember Me* and *All Our Wounds Forgiven* for fictional meditations on the African American condition in American society and the nonfictional *Falling Pieces of the Broken Sky*. Patricia Williams, *The Alchemy of Race and Rights: Diary of a Law Professor* and *The Rooster's Egg* analyze the state of African America and American society from the perspective of law, especially the area known as critical race theory. One of the major proponents of this school of thought is Richard Delgado. See, for example, *The Rodrigo Chronicles*. Toni Morrison also writes both fiction and nonfiction. See, for example, two of her most highly acclaimed fictional works, *Song of Solomon* (1977) and *Beloved* (1987). In the area of nonfiction, see her *Playing in the Dark*. For strictly nonfiction analyses and commentaries, see Kelley, *Race Rebels*. Bell hooks is one of the leading black women intellectuals who have written on feminism. See her *Killing Rage: Ending Racism*. See also Michele Wallace, *Invisibility Blues*. For conservative analyses, see Loury, *One by One from the Inside Out*. Two essays that cut across ideological grounds and attempt to present fresh ideas can be found in Rivers, "On the Responsibility of Intellectuals in the Age of Crack," and "Beyond the Nationalism of Fools: Toward an Agenda for Black Intellectuals." 54. Gates and West, *The Future of the Race*. For more insights from a variety of black intellectuals on the Du Boisian double-consciousness theorem, see Early, ed., *Lure and Loathing*. Gates has an essay therein entitled "The Welcome Table," 144–63. The reception of this work was modest. See Early, "Black Like Them." Early felt that the essays seemed "honestly written" but that "the very Victorian idea of a social mission described in the 1903 essay . . . is still compelling, still worth emulating." But see also Painter, "A Different Sense of Time," who stated that black women's studies was "likely to find more grounds for hope in the future of the race than the future of the race."

55. Gates and West, *The Future of the Race*, xii. All other pages quoted are cited in the text.

56. See Frazier, *The Negro in the United States*; Cox, *Caste, Race, and Class*; Ladner, *The Death of White Sociology*; Elijah Anderson, *Streetwise: Race, Class, and Change in an Urban Community*. On William Julius Wilson, see his *The Declining Significance of Race*, *The Truly Disadvantaged*, and *When Work Disappears: The World of the New Urban Poor*. An insightful profile of Wilson can be found in Remnick, "Dr. Wilson's Neighborhood." On white sociologists who influenced black thinkers, see Dollard, *Caste and Class in a Southern Town*. For a perceptive reading of Robert Ezra Park, see Vernon Williams, *Re-Thinking Race*, chapter 5.

57. See Quarles, *The Negro in the Making of America*.

58. On this matter, see Moses, *The Golden Age of Black Nationalism*, chapter 5, for a discussion of this movement as well as Gaines, *Uplifting the Race*, 130–31, and Paula Giddings, *When and Where I Enter*.

59. See Lewis, *Du Bois: Biography of a Race*, 248–51, 567–79, and 574–78. On Du Bois and Garvey, see Lewis's *When Harlem Was in Vogue*, 37–44. An excellent overview of black nationalism is provided in Moses, ed., *Classical Black Nationalism: From the American Revolution to Marcus Garvey*, 1–42.

60. See Moses, *Classical Black Nationalism*.

61. Thomas Holt made a similar observation regarding black historians in the mid-1980s. See his "Whither Now and Why." Holt's assessment is more plausible than what Gates and West are driving at. In a similar vein, see Meier and Rudwick, *Black History and the Historical Profession, 1915–1980*.

62. Kilson, "Colin Powell: A Flight from Power?"

3. The Conservative Revolution and Its Impact on Afro America, 1980–1992

1. A good biographical sketch of George Schuyler upon which I have drawn is the entry by Robert Fay in *Microsoft Encarta Africana*. Even better, however, is Oscar R. Williams, *George S. Schuyler: Portrait of a Black Conservative*. Williams's research suggests that Schuyler was more of an upstate New Yorker than he let on and his actual birthplace is a mystery.

2. Gates, "A Fragmented Man: George Schuyler and the Claims of Race," 5 (page numbers refer to the article at http://nytimes.com).

3. Fay, "Schuyler, George S." Schuyler recounts meeting Josephine Cogdell in his autobiography *Black and Conservative*, 163–64. His and Josephine's raising of their daughter Phillipa Duke Schuyler is discussed on pages 251–53. Phillipa's biography has been done by Talalay, *Composition in Black and White: The Life of Phillipa Schuyler*.

4. Schuyler, *Black and Conservative*, 163–64; Fay, "Schuyler, George S."

5. Schuyler, "The Negro Art Hokum," 96–99. The quote in the text is from Schuyler, *Black and Conservative*, 157.

6. Schuyler, *Black and Conservative*, 121.

7. Gates, "A Fragmented Man," 2.

8. Ibid., 4–6.

9. Ibid., 4.

10. See Hemenway, *Zora Neale Hurston: A Literary Biography*. Hemenway's biography remains the standard treatment. But for an example of reinventiveness, see Hurston, *Dust Tracks on the Road*. Ralph Ellison's work is ably discussed in Watts, *Heroism and the Black Intellectual*.

11. Hurston, "How It Feels to Be Colored Me," 215–16.

12. Hemenway, *Zora Neale Hurston*, 347–48; Alice Walker, *In My Mother's Garden*.

13. Hemenway, *Zora Heale Hurston*, 329 and 336; for Schuyler's views on the Civil Rights movement, see his *Black and Conservative*, chapter 19.

14. Hurston, *Dust Tracks on the Road*, 162–65.

15. Memoirs reconstructing his move from left to right are in *A Personal Odyssey* and *A Man of Letters* (http//www.townhall.com/columnists/bio). See also an extensive interview of Sowell in http://www.salon.com/books/int/1999/11/10/sowell/index.html.

16. Interview, http://www.salon.com.

17. Banner-Haley, *The Fruits of Integration*, chapter 3.

18. Weisbrot, *Freedom Bound*, 295. For a rebuttal of this position from the Left, see Dyson, *I May Not Get There with You: The True Martin Luther King, Jr.*, 12–14.

19. Sitkoff, *Struggle for Black Equality*, 214–15.

20. Ibid., 215–18; Weisbrot, *Freedom Bound*, 301–5; Franklin and Moss, *From Slavery to Freedom*, 512; O'Reilly, *Nixon's Piano*, 335–50 and chapter 9.

21. Sitkoff, *Struggle for Black Equality*, 227–28; Weisbrot, *Freedom Bound*, 310–11; Franklin and Moss, *From Slavery to Freedom*, 539.

22. Gilder, *Wealth and Poverty*.

23. Charles Murray, *Losing Ground*.

24. Loury, *One by One from the Inside Out*; Sowell, *The Economics and Politics of Race*; and *Barbarians Inside the Gates*. Randall Kennedy's ideas are detailed in Jim Sleeper, *Liberal Racism*, chapter 6, 118–35.

25. See Loury, *One by One from the Inside Out*, chapters 2 and 4. The two best recent works on the Nation of Islam are Clegg, *An Original Man: The Life and Times of Elijah Muhammad* and Evanzz, *The Messenger: The Rise and Fall of Elijah Muhammad*.

26. It was a long-standing policy of the Nation of Islam to refrain from participating in the political process principally because of the Honorable Elijah Muhammad's belief that the "white devils" had corrupted the system. See Clegg, *An Original Man*, as well as Evanzz, *The Messenger*.

27. Clegg, *An Original Man*; Evanzz, *The Messenger*.

28. Franklin and Moss, *From Slavery to Freedom*, 539–40; Sitkoff, *Struggle for Black Equality*, 222–23; Weisbrot, *Freedom Bound*, 313–14.

29. Franklin and Moss, 540. An excellent analysis of Jesse Jackson's political career can be found in Reed, *The Jesse Jackson Phenomenon*.

30. Franklin and Moss, *From Slavery to Freedom*, 542. A good overview of Farrakhan and his activities in this period can be found in Hine, Hine, and Harrold, *The African-American Odyssey*, 581–83.

31. Farrakhan's remarks about Judaism can be found in Bird, "Church and Civil Rights Groups Assail New Remark by Farrakhan," A22. See also Hine, Hine, and Harrold, *African-American Odyssey*, 581–83. Khallid Abdul Muhammad's remarks were made at Kean College in New Jersey in 1993. He was then a top aide to Farrakhan.

32. Lester, "The Time Has Come, 11–12; Gates, "Black Demagogues and Pseudo-Scholars." Derrick Bell and Martin Kilson were among those black intellectuals who felt it was unnecessary to denounce everything that Farrakhan said. See Bell, *Faces of the Bottom of the Well*, and Martin Kilson, "The Interaction of the Black Mainstream Leadership and the Farrakhan Extremists," 238–45.

33. Quote taken from Glennon, *Our Times*, 605–6.

34. Ali, *The Black Man's Guide to Understanding the Black Woman*; Clegg, *An Original Man*, and Evanzz, *The Messenger*.

35. See Lena Williams, "Black Women's Book Starts a Predictable Storm," C14–15.

36. An excellent analysis of Farrakhan and these matters is Reed, "The Rise of Louis Farrakhan."

37. Franklin and Moss, *From Slavery to Freedom,* 541, for a picture of the more prominent black mayors. Hine, Hine, and Harrold, *African-American Odyssey,* 545–46 and 572–73, for an historical overview of black elected officials.

38. Franklin and Moss, *From Slavery to Freedom,* 533–35, offers full coverage of this incident. See also Hine, Hine, and Harrold, *African-American Odyssey,* 567.

39. Franklin and Moss, *From Slavery to Freedom,* 533–35.

40. Franklin and Moss, *From Slavery to Freedom,* 535–38; Hine, Hine, and Harrold, *African-American Odyssey,* 570–72, provide a good general overview of affirmative action and the blacklash. See also O'Reilly, *Nixon's Piano,* 362.

41. Franklin and Moss, *From Slavery to Freedom,* 538–39. It should be noted that the unemployment rate for African Americans was more than twice that of whites: 18.9 percent.

42. O'Reilly, *Nixon's Piano,* 357–58.

43. Ibid., 359.

44. Ibid., 360.

45. Faragher et al., *Out of Many,* 983–84.

46. O'Reilly, *Nixon's Piano,* 361–62. But see also Dyson, *I May Not Go There with You,* 12–14 and 25–29.

47. Steele, *The Content of Our Character.* Steele followed up this book of essays with another: *A Dream Deferred.* See chapter 1, "The Loneliness of the Black Conservative," in particular. He continued this exposition with *White Guilt.*

48. Loury, *One by One;* Steele, *Content of Our Character* and *A Dream Deferred.*

49. Ibid.

50. On uplift ideology, see Gaines, *Uplifting the Race,* introduction and chapter 1.

51. C. West, "Parents and National Survival" and "On the 1980s," details the nihilism mentioned above. On Robert Woodson, see Banner-Haley, *Fruits of Integration,* 74. On Eugene Rivers, see the sources in note 59.

52. Rivers, "Beyond the Nationalism of Fools," 16–18, summarizes his views. See also the follow-up replies by a number of noted black and white intellectuals in "Readers Forum: Replies to Eugene Rivers' 'Nationalism of Fools.'" The argument that caught most black and white intellectuals' attention was Eugene Rivers III, "On the Responsibility of Intellectuals in the Age of Crack."

53. Cose et al., "The Good News about Black America."

54. Most of my information on Thomas is taken from O'Reilly, *Nixon's Piano,* 395–99. But see also Hine, Hine, and Harrold, *The African-American Odyssey,* 567–69.

55. O'Reilly, *Nixon's Piano,* 396.

56. Ibid., 397–98.

57. Ibid., 397–98. See also Hine, Hine, and Harrold, *The African-American Odyssey,* 568.

58. Glenn C. Loury is another example of this conservative integrationist nationalism. See his *One by One* and chapter 8 in Jim Sleeper's *Liberal Racism.* For an admiring assessment of Thomas's first ten years on the Supreme Court, see Mauro, "Thomas Makes His Mark."

59. West and Gates, *The Future of the Race,* explore this shift in its introduction. For a critique of Thomas, see Higginbotham, "Justice Clarence Thomas in Retrospect."

4. Popular Culture and the African American
Intellectual Search for a New American Identity

1. The chain of events in the novel is based on the Presidential Succession Act of 1947. A new succession act came into being in the 1970s that would have invalidated Wallace's plotline. Information on Irving Wallace (1916–1990) can be found in Leverence, *Irving Wallace: A Writer's Profile.*

2. Ellison, *Shadow and Act.* On Ellison's political shift, see Rampersad, *Ralph Ellison: A Biography*, chapter 6.

3. Douglass, "Composite Nation," 1869. The complete text can be found at http://BlackPast.org.

4. Ellison's leftist associations and integrationist thinking are cogently presented in Rampersad, *Ralph Ellison*, chapters 4–6. The complete text can be found in Foner and Rosenberg, eds., *Racism, Dissent, and Asian-Americans from 1850 to the Present.*

5. See Watts, *Heroism and the Black Intellectual*; Banner-Haley, "Ralph Ellison and the Invisibility of the Black Intellectual"; and Warren, "Ralph Ellison and the Problem of Cultural Authority: The Lessons of Little Rock."

6. For extensive detail of the fire, see Rampersad, *Ralph Ellison*, chapter 17. The full text of *Juneteenth* will eventually be published by the Library of America as provided by John Callahan.

7. See Rampersad, *Ralph Ellison*, chapters 16–19. As stated in n. 6 the full text of Ellison's novel in progress with annotations will eventually appear.

8. Lester, *To Be a Slave*; Morrison, *Song of Solomon.* See also Charles Johnson, *Oxherding Tale*, which is closer to the artistic values that Ellison espoused.

9. Genovese, *Roll, Jordan, Roll*; Gutman, *The Black Family in Slavery and Freedom, 1725–1925*; Levine, *Black Culture and Black Consciousness*; Blassingame, *The Slave Community*; White, *Ar'n't I a Woman: Female Slaves in the Plantation South.*

10. Morrison, *Playing in the Dark*, 52.

11. Ibid., 65. Lester, *To Be a Slave*; Owens, *This Species of Property;* but more pointedly, see Owens's essay "The African in the Garden: New World Slavery and Its Lifelines"; Harding, *There Is a River*; and Stuckey, *Slave Culture.*

12. Morrison, *Beloved*; Watts, *Heroism and the Black Intellectual*, 107. On Ellison's connection to nineteenth-century literary figures, see Lawrence Jackson, *Ralph Ellison*, 196, 396–97, and Rampersad, *Ralph Ellison*, 192, 195–97.

13. Lester, *And All Our Wounds Forgiven.*

14. Watts points out that "Ellison viewed blacks as 'omni-Americans,' a concept expounded on by Albert Murray." Murray was a close friend of Ellison's since their college days at Tuskegee Institute. Murray's book, *The Omni-Americans*, is a smart and rigorous reinforcement of Ralph Ellison's thought albeit from a more culturally conservative standpoint. See also Baldwin, *The Fire Next Time.*

15. Century, "Setting the Civil Rights Record Straight," 10.

16. Ibid.

17. Lewis, *W. E. B. Du Bois: The Fight for Equality and the American Century*, 176–77, on the "Criteria of Negro Art"; Smethurst, "The Adventures of a Social Poet"; Rowley, *Richard Wright*, 136–38, for "Blueprint for Negro Writing"; Rampersad, *Ralph Ellison*, chapter 5.

18. Nikhil Pal Singh, "Negro Exceptionalism: The Antinomies of Harold Cruse," 80; Rampersad, *Ralph Ellison*, chapter 5; Gaines, *American Africans in Africa.*

19. See Singh on the black nationality formulation in "Negro Exceptionalism" and *Black Is a Country*, chapter 2. As for Du Bois, see *Souls of Black Folks*, "Of Our Spiritual Strivings."

20. Singh, *Black Is a Country*, chapter 1; Rampersad, *Langston Hughes*, vol. 1, chapters 3–7; Lewis, *When Harlem Was in Vogue*, 170–75.

21. Ward, *Just My Soul Responding*, parts 1–2.

22. See Ward, *Just My Soul Responding*, 142–56, for brilliant analysis of the black pop era and its biracialism. Subsequent references to this work will be made parenthetically in the text.

23. Ward, *Just My Soul Responding*, 258–68; Cecil Brown, "James Brown, Hoo-doo, and Black Culture," 189–95; Banner-Haley, *Fruits of Integration*, chapter 5.

24. The best biography of Jimi Hendrix that places him in a full context of his times is Henderson, *'Scuse Me While I Kiss the Sky*. See also Ward, *Just My Soul Responding*, 244–48, for insightful analysis on the racial politics of Hendrix's music.

25. George, *Post-Soul Nation*, ix.

26. Ibid.; Banner-Haley, *Fruits of Integration*, chapter 1; Holloway, *Confronting the Veil*.

27. George, *Post-Soul Nation*, x. A general start at understanding the underclass is Katz, ed., *The "Underclass" Debate*; Kete outlines his theory of Afrocentricity in the *Afrocentric Idea*, but see a more nuanced examination in Moses, *Afrotopia*. For critiques of race essentialism, see Dyson, *Reflecting Black*, and Kelley, *Freedom Dreams*.

28. Alice Walker defines "womanist" in the preface of her book of essays, *In Search of Our Mothers' Gardens*. On Zora Neale Hurston, see Walker, "Looking for Zora," and Hemenway, *Zora Neale Hurston*. Finally, *The Color Purple* was made into a motion picture directed by Steven Spielberg and starring Whoopi Goldberg, Oprah Winfrey, and Danny Glover.

29. Steele, *White Guilt*, 5–6.

30. McWhorter, "Still Losing the Race," 37. McWhorter produced a more detailed explanation of the white leftist ruination of blacks in *Winning the Race*.

31. For example, see Gates's discussion in Gates and West, *The Future of the Race*.

32. McWhorter, "Still Losing the Race," 37; Bloom, *The Closing of the American Mind*.

33. D'Sousa, *The End of Racism*; Herrnstein and Murray, *The Bell Curve*.

34. Michael K. Brown et al., *Whitewashing Race*.

35. Baldwin, *The Fire Next Time*. For an overview of Baldwin's oeuvre, see *The Price of the Ticket*; Gaines, *American Africans in Africa*.

36. Smethurst, *The Black Arts Movement*.

37. Alice Walker, *The Color Purple* and *In Search of Our Mothers' Gardens*; Jordan, *Affirmative Acts*; Morrison, *Song of Solomon*; Angelou, *I Know Why the Caged Bird Sings*; Carby, *Reconstructing Black Womanhood*; Collins, *Black Sexual Politics*; hooks, *Ain't I a Woman*; Patricia Williams, *The Alchemy of Race*.

38. Singh, *Black Is a Country*, 11. By 2007, with the Supreme Court decision knocking down the use of race to integrate schools, this assessment was painfully realized.

39. See a sampling of Thomas Nast's work at http://cartoons.osu.edu/nast/.

40. Strömberg, *Black Images in the Comics*.

41. Banner-Haley, *To Do Good and to Do Well*, 93; Jeffrey A. Brown, *Black Superheroes*.

42. See "Ollie" Harrington's commentaries and cartoons in Harrington and Inge, eds., *Why I Left America and Other Essays,* and Harrington and Inge, eds., *Dark Laughter: The Satiric Art of Oliver W. Harrington.*

43. Savage, *Commies, Cowboys, and Jungle Queens,* 84–94. An article on how integration in the comics from 1954 to 1999 was presented and what that meant for a shift in white liberal anticommunist sensibilities is forthcoming from Banner-Haley, "We Are All One Together: Race, Nation, and Integration in the Comics, 1954–1999."

44. Savage, *Commies, Cowboys, and Jungle Queens,* chapter 6; Pierce, "What Is Not So Funny about the Funnies," 55.

45. For examples of the comic strips mentioned, see http://www.comics.com. On Milestone/DC, see Jeffery Brown, *Black Superheroes;* Carolyn M. Brown, "Marketing a New Universe of Heroes."

46. The biographical material is culled from McGrath, "The Radical." For a good sampling of strips, articles, and interviews with McGruder that assess the impact of his work, see Aaron McGruder, *All the Rage.*

5. A New Century and New Challenges: The Visibility of African American Intellectuals and the Construction of Diasporic Diversity

1. See M. West's *The Education of Booker T. Washington* for an excellent analysis of Washington's intellectual contribution to the flawed concept of race relations. Gaines's *Uplifting the Race* offers illuminating analyses of how African American intellectuals fared. Of course see Lewis's magisterial two-volume biography of W. E. B. Du Bois.

2. On Anna Julia Cooper, see the collection of her writings, Lemert, ed., *The Voice of Anna Julia Cooper;* an excellent analysis of Alice Dunbar Nelson can be found in Gaines, *Uplifting the Race,* chapter 3. Modern black feminist intellectuals have been highly productive. A sample would include Patricia Williams, *The Rooster's Egg;* hooks, *Ain't I a Woman;* Jordan, *And Some of Us Did Not Die;* Collins, *Black Feminist Thought;* Alice Walker, *In Search of Our Mothers' Gardens.*

3. See, for example, Hall, "What Is This 'Black' in Black Popular Culture?"; Gilroy, *The Black Atlantic,* and Carby, *Race Men.* The controversy on gender can be seen in Patterson's essay, "Blacklash." Black and white intellectuals responded to this essay in *Transition* 66 (1995), 73–163. Also see Patterson, *The Ordeal of Integration.*

4. See *Transition* 1, no. 1 (1990).

5. See, for example, *Reconstruction* 1, no. 3 (1996).

6. See M. Brown et al., *Whitewashing Race.*

7. See Marable, *Race, Reform, and Rebellion,* chapters 9 and 10.

8. See for example Holt, *The Problem of Race in the Twenty-First Century,* and Dyson, *Debating Race.*

9. The *New Yorker* issue on black America (February 25, 1995) was edited by Henry Louis Gates Jr. and Hendrik Hertzberg. Gates's *Thirteen Ways of Looking at a Black Man* is a compilation of his *New Yorker* columns.

10. Bradley, *Harvard Rules,* 85–124.

11. Cosmopolitanism is richly explored in Appiah, *Cosmopolitanism.*

12. On West and Summers, see Bradley, *Harvard Rules,* 85–124; and Tanenhaus, "The Ivy League's Angry Star," 200–203, 218–23.

13. See Cornel West, *Prophetic Fragments.* On Richard Rorty, see, for example, Rorty, *Philosophy and Social Hope,* and Brandom, ed., *Rorty and His Critics.*

14. Wieseltier, "All and Nothing at All," 31.

15. For example, see Bradley, *Harvard Rules,* 99–100; Tanenhaus, "The Ivy League's Angry Star," 219–20.

16. Bradley, *Harvard Rules,* 92–93; Tanenhaus, "The Ivy League's Angry Star," 203.

17. Ibid.; Cornel West, *Race Matters.*

18. "After 371 Years, Harvard Plans to Name First Female President," *New York Times,* 10 Feb. 2007, A1, A11; Robib Wilson, "The Power of Professors," *Chronicle of Higher Education,* 3 Mar. 2006, A10–13.

19. West and hooks, *Breaking Bread.* West's first spoken-word recording was entitled *Sketches of My Culture* (2001). He made another rap CD in 2007, *Never Forget: A Journey of Revelations.*

20. On Arthur Jensen, see Miele, *Intelligence, Race, and Genetics: Conversations with Arthur R. Jensen;* Herrnstein and Murray, *The Bell Curve.*

21. See Hotchkin, "Henry Louis Gates Stays at Harvard."

22. Dyson, *Race Rules,* 56.

23. Charles Johnson, *Turning the Wheel,* 92.

24. *Jet,* 27 July 1992, 27.

25. Obama, *Dreams from My Father,* covers Obama's life in rich and eloquent detail. Also see New York Times, *Obama: The Historic Journey,* 32–38.

26. Obama, *Dreams from My Father,* 134.

27. Resolution of SNCC in Kai Wright, ed., *The African American Experience,* 506.

28. Obama, *Dreams from My Father;* New York Times, *Obama,* 40.

29. New York Times, *Obama,* 48–50; Obama, *Dreams from My Father,* 438–40.

30. Ibid. On Thurgood Marshall, see Juan Williams, *Thurgood Marshall, American Revolutionary;* McNeil, *Groundwork;* Randall Kennedy, *Race, Crime, and the Law;* Guinier, *Lift Every Voice.*

31. New York Times, *Obama,* 52–53.

32. Ibid. Some of those new politicians were Corey Booker from Newark, NJ (mayor); Jesse Jackson Jr. (congressman from Illinois); Deval Patrick, Massachusetts (governor). These were all Democrats. A Republican example would be Michael Steele (lt. governor of Maryland).

33. New York Times, *Obama,* 58.

34. "Keynote Address by Barack Obama to the Democratic National Convention 27 July 2004," in Obama, *Dreams from My Father,* 457.

35. New York Times, *Obama,* 61.

36. William Julius Wilson, *The Declining Significance of Race.* For a critique of this book see Lester, "The Mark of Race," 115–18. A more recent elaboration of Wilson's thinking can be found in *More than Just Race.*

37. Dickerson, "Colorblind."

38. Ibid.

39. Ibid.

40. Lester, "Black Racism."

41. Lester, "Why Black Americans Are Indebted to White Americans."

42. Charles Johnson, "The End of the Black American Narrative."

43. Early, "The End of Race as We Know It," 11.

44. Charles Johnson, "The End of the Black American Narrative," 39–40.

45. Barack Obama, "A More Perfect Union," in New York Times, *Obama*, 105 and 106.

46. Obama, "More Perfect Union," 108.

47. The black Left certainly seemed satisfied. See, for example, Cornel West, *Hope on a Tightrope*, 57–61. But black conservatives were not convinced. See Steele, *A Bound Man.*

48. Patterson, "The Eternal Revolution," A35; Gates, "Integration at the Top"; Alice Walker, "White House Advice," 106–08; Lester, "The Inauguration."

49. The notion of "transformative intellectuals" is Du Boisian and is elaborated on in Watts, "The Souls of Black Folks and Afro-American Intellectual Life." I am indebted to the Watts essay for my own thoughts here.

Bibliography

"After 371 Years, Harvard Plans to Name First Female President." *New York Times*, 10 Feb. 2007, A1, A11.

Ali, Scheherazade. *The Black Man's Guide to Understanding the Black Woman*. Philadelphia: Civilized Publications, 1989.

Anderson, Elijah. *Streetwise: Race, Class, and Change in an Urban Community*. Chicago: U of Chicago P, 1990.

Anderson, James D. *The Education of Blacks in the South, 1860–1935*. Chapel Hill: U of North Carolina P, 1988.

Angelou, Maya. *I Know Why the Caged Bird Sings*. New York: Random House, 1969.

Appiah, Kwame Anthony. *Cosmopolitanism: Ethics in a World of Strangers*. New York: W. W. Norton, 2006.

Baldwin, James. *The Fire Next Time*. New York: Dial, 1963.

———. *The Price of the Ticket: Collected Nonfiction, 1948–1985*. New York: St. Martin's, 1985.

Banks, William. *Black Intellectuals*. New York: W. W. Norton, 1996.

Banner-Haley, Charles Pete T. *The Fruits of Integration: Black Middle Class Ideology and Culture, 1960–1990*. Jackson: UP of Mississippi, 1994.

———. "Ralph Ellison and the Invisibility of the Black Intellectual: Historical Reflections on *Invisible Man*." Chapter 8 in Morel, *Ralph Ellison and the Raft of Hope*.

———. *To Do Good and to Do Well: Middle Class Blacks and the Depression, Philadelphia, 1929–1941*. New York: Garland, 1993.

Bell, Derrick. *Faces of the Bottom of the Well: The Permanence of Racism*. New York: Basic Books, 1992.

Bird, David. "Church and Civil Rights Groups Assail New Remark by Farrakhan." *New York Times*, 28 June 1984, A22.

Black, Edwin. *War against the Weak: Eugenics and America's Campaign to Create a Master Class*. New York: Dialog Press, 2003.

Blassingame, John. *The Slave Community: Plantation Life in the Antebellum South*. New York: Oxford UP, 1972, 1979.

Bloom, Allan. *The Closing of the American Mind*. New York: Simon and Schuster, 1985.

Borstelmann, Thomas. *The Cold War and the Color Line: American Race Relations in the Global Arena*. Cambridge, MA: Harvard UP, 2001.

Boyd, Valerie. *Wrapped in Rainbows: A Life of Zora Neale Hurston*. London: Virago, 2003.

Bradley, Richard. *Harvard Rules: The Struggle for the Soul of the World's Most Powerful University*. New York: HarperCollins, 2005.

Branch, Taylor. *Parting the Waters: America in the King Years: 1954–63*. New York: Simon and Schuster, 1988.

Brandom, Robert B., ed., *Rorty and His Critics*. New York: Blackwell, 2000.

Brown, Carolyn M. "Marketing a New Universe of Heroes." *Black Enterprise*, November 1994, 80–88.

Brown, Cecil. "James Brown, Hoodoo, and Black Culture." In *Black Review #1*. 189–95. Edited by Mel Watkins. New York: William Morrow, 1971.

Brown, Jeffrey A. *Black Superheroes: Milestone Comics and Their Fans*. Jackson: UP of Mississippi, 2001.

Brown, Michael K., et al. *Whitewashing Race: The Myth of a Color-Blind Society*. Berkeley: U of California P, 2003.

Buni, Andrew. *Robert L. Vann of the Pittsburgh Courier: Politics and Black Journalism*. Pittsburgh: U of Pittsburgh P, 1974.

Butchart, Ronald E. *Northern Schools, Southern Blacks, and Reconstruction: Freedman's Education, 1862–1875*. Westport, CT: Greenwood, 1980.

Callahan, John F., ed. *The Collected Essays of Ralph Ellison*. New York: Modern Library, 1995.

Carby, Hazel V. *Race Men*. Cambridge, MA: Harvard UP, 1998.

———. *Reconstructing Womanhood: The Emergence of the Afro-American Woman Novelist*. New York: Oxford UP, 1987.

Carmichael, Stokely, and Charles V. Hamilton. *Black Power: The Politics of Liberation in America*. New York: Random House, 1967.

Carson, Clayborne. *In Struggle: SNCC and the Black Awakening of the Sixties*. Cambridge: Harvard UP, 1982.

Carson, Clayborne, et al. *Reporting Civil Rights: Part One: American Journalism, 1941–1963*. New York: Library of America, 2003.

Century, Douglas. "Setting the Civil Rights Record Straight." *Forward*, 24 June 1994, 10.

Cleaver, Eldridge. *Soul on Ice*. New York: McGraw-Hill, 1968.

Clegg, Claude, III. *An Original Man: The Life and Times of Elijah Muhammad*. New York: St. Martin's, 1997.

Collins, Patricia Hill. *Black Feminist Thought: Knowledge, Consciousness, and the Politics of Empowerment*. 2nd ed. New York: Routledge, 1999.

———. *Black Sexual Politics: African Americans, Gender, and the New Racism*. New York: Routledge, 2004.

Cose, Ellis, et al. "The Good News about Black America—And Why Many Blacks Aren't Celebrating." *Newsweek*, 7 June 1999, 28–40.

Cox, Oliver C. *Caste, Class, and Race: A Study in Social Dynamics*. Garden City, NY: Doubleday, 1948. Reprint, with an introduction by Adolph Reed Jr. New York: Monthly Review, 2000.

Cruse, Harold. *The Crisis of the Negro Intellectual*. New York: William Morrow, 1967. Reprint, New York: NYRB Classics, 2005.

Dagbovie, Pero Gaglo. *The Early Black History Movement, Carter G. Woodson, and Lorenzo Johnston Greene*. Urbana: U of Illinois P, 2007.

Delgado, Richard. *The Rodrigo Chronicles: Conversations about America and Race*. New York: New York UP, 1995.

Denning, Michael. *The Cultural Front*. Brooklyn, NY: Verso, 1998.

Dickerson, Debra J. "Colorblind." Opinion. Salon.com. 22 Jan. 2007. http://www.salon.com/opinion/feature/2007/01/22/obama/index.html.

Dollard, John. *Caste and Class in a Southern Town*. 1937. Madison: U of Wisconsin P, 1987.

Douglass, Frederick. "Composite Nation," 1869. http://BlackPast.org.

Drake, St. Clair, and Horace R. Cayton. *Black Metropolis: A Study of Negro Life in a Northern City*. 1945. Chicago: U of Chicago P, 1993.

D'Sousa, Dinesh. *The End of Racism: Principles for a Multiracial Society*. New York: Free Press, 1995.

Du Bois, W. E. B. "The Negro and Communism." *The Crisis* (1931). Reprinted in Lewis, *W. E. B. Du Bois: A Reader*, 583–93.

———. "Separation and Self-Respect," *The Crisis* (1934). Reprinted in Lewis, *W. E. B. Du Bois: A Reader*, 559.

———. *The Souls of Black Folk*. 1903. New York: Oxford UP, 2009.

Dudziak, Mary. *Cold War Civil Rights: Race and the Image of American Democracy*. Princeton, NJ: Princeton UP, 2002.

Dyson, Michael Eric. *Debating Race: With Michael Eric Dyson*. New York: Basic Civitas Books, 2007.

———. *I May Not Get There with You: The True Martin Luther King, Jr*. New York: Free Press, 2000.

———. *Race Rules: Navigating the Color Line*. New York: Basic Books, 1996.

———. *Reflecting Black: African-American Cultural Criticism*. Minneapolis: U of Minnesota P, 1993.

Early, Gerald. "Black Like Them." Rev. of *The Future of the Race*, by Henry Louis Gates Jr. and Cornel West. *New York Times Book Review*, 21 April 1996, 1.

———. "The End of Race as We Know It." *Chronicle Review* 55, no. 7 (10 October 2008): B11.

Early, Gerald., ed. *Lure and Loathing: Essays on Race, Identity, and the Ambivalence of Assimilation*. New York: Penguin, 1993.

Egerton, John. *Speak Now against the Day: The Generation before the Civil Rights Movement in the South*. New York: Alfred A. Knopf, 1994.

Ellison, Ralph. "*An American Dilemma*: A Review." In *Shadow and Act*. Reprinted in Callahan, 328–40. New York: Modern Library, 1995.

———. *Invisible Man*. 1952. New York: Vintage, 1995.

———. *Juneteenth: A Novel*. New York: Random House, 1999.

———. *Shadow and Act*. New York: Vintage Books, 1964.

Evans, Richard J. *The Coming of the Third Reich*. New York: Penguin, 2003.

———. *The Third Reich in Power*. New York: Penguin, 2005.

Evanzz, Karl. *The Messenger: The Rise and Fall of Elijah Muhammad*. New York: Random House, 2000.

Fabre, Michel. *The Unfinished Quest of Richard Wright*. 2d ed. Urbana: U of Illinois P, 1993.

Fanon, Frantz. *The Wretched of the Earth*. New York: Grove, 1966.

Faragher, Jack Mack, et al. *Out of Many: A History of the American People, 1850–1920*. Upper Saddle River, NJ: Prentice Hall, 1995, 1999, 2001, 2005, 2008.

Fay, Robert. "Schuyler, George S." *Microsoft Encarta Africana*. Microsoft Corporation, 1999.

Foner, Philip S., and Daniel Rosenberg, eds. *Racism, Dissent, and Asian Americans from 1850 to the Present: A Documentary History*. Westport, CT: Greenwood, 1993.

Franklin, John Hope, and Alfred A. Moss Jr. *From Slavery to Freedom: A History of African Americans.* 8th ed. New York: Knopf, 2000.

Frazier, E. Franklin. *Black Bourgeoisie.* Glencoe, IL: Free Press of Glencoe, 1957; New York: Simon and Schuster, Free Press, 1997.

———. "Le Bourgeoisie Noir," in *African American Mosaic,* vol. 2, edited by John Bracey and Manisha Sinha, 201–6. Upper Saddle River, NJ: Prentice Hall, 2004.

———. *The Negro Family in the United States.* Chicago: U of Chicago P, 1939.

———. *The Negro in the United States.* New York: Macmillan, 1957.

Gaines, Kevin K. *American Africans in Africa.* Chapel Hill: U of North Carolina P, 2006.

———. *Uplifting the Race: Black Leadership, Politics, and Culture in the Twentieth Century.* Chapel Hill: U of North Carolina P, 1996.

Gates, Henry Louis, Jr. "Black Demagogues and Pseudo-Scholars." *New York Times,* op. ed., 20 July 1992, A15.

———. "A Fragmented Man: George Schuyler and the Claims of Race." *New York Times Book Review* (Sunday), 20 September 1992, 5. (Page numbers refer to the article at http://nytimes.com).

———. *Thirteen Ways of Looking at a Black Man.* New York: Random House, 1997.

———. "The Welcome Table." In Early, *Lure and Loathing,* 144–63.

Gates, Henry Louis, Jr., and Hendrik Hertzberg, eds. Issue on Black America. *New Yorker,* 25 Feb. 1995.

Gates, Henry Louis, Jr., and Cornel West. *The Future of the Race.* New York: Alfred A. Knopf, 1996.

Genovese, Eugene D. *Roll, Jordan, Roll: The World the Slaves Made.* New York: Pantheon, 1974.

George, Nelson. *Post-Soul Nation: The Explosive, Contradictory, Triumphant, and Tragic 1980s as Experienced by African Americans (Previously Known as Blacks and Before That Negroes).* New York: Viking, 2004.

Gilder, George. *Wealth and Poverty.* New York: Basic Books, 1981.

Gilmore, Glenda Elizabeth. *Defying Dixie: The Radical Roots of Civil Rights, 1919–1950.* New York: W. W. Norton, 2008.

Gilroy, Paul. *The Black Atlantic: Modernity and Double Consciousness.* Cambridge, MA: Harvard UP, 1993.

Glennon, Lorraine, ed. *Our Times: An Illustrated History of the 20th Century.* Atlanta, GA: Turner Publishing, 1995.

Goggin, Jacqueline. *Carter G. Woodson: A Life in Black History.* Baton Rouge: Louisiana State UP, 1993.

Guerl, Matthew Pratt. *The Color of Race in America, 1900–1940.* Cambridge, MA: Harvard UP, 2001.

Guinier, Lani. *Lift Every Voice: Turning a Civil Rights Setback into a Vision of Social Justice.* New York: Simon and Schuster, 1998.

Gutman, Herbert. *The Black Family in Slavery and Freedom, 1725–1925.* New York: Pantheon, 1976.

Guy-Sheftall, Beverly, ed. *Words of Fire: An Anthology of African-American Feminist Thought.* New York: New Press, 1995.

Hagan, Wesley C. *Many Minds, One Heart: SNCC's Dream for a New America.* Chapel Hill: U of North Carolina P, 2007.

Hall, Stuart. "What Is This 'Black' in Black Popular Culture?" In *The Black Studies Reader,* edited by Jacqueline Bobo, Cynthia Hudley, and Claudine Michel, 255–65. New York: Routledge, 2004.

Harding, Vincent. *There Is a River: The Black Struggle for Freedom in America.* New York: Harcourt, 1981.

Harrington, Oliver W. *Why I Left America and Other Essays.* Jackson: UP of Mississippi, 1994.

Harrington, Oliver W., and M. Thomas Inge, ed. *Dark Laughter: The Satiric Art of Oliver W. Harrington: From the Walter O. Evans Collection of African American Art.* Jackson: UP of Mississippi, 1993.

Hemenway, Robert E. *Zora Neale Hurston: A Literary Biography.* Urbana: U of Illinois P, 1977.

Henderson, David. *Jimi Hendrix: Voodoo Child of the Aquarian Age.* New York: Doubleday, 1978. Condensed and revised as *'Scuse Me While I Kiss the Sky: The Life of Jimi Hendrix,* Bantam, 1981. Reprint, New York: Atria, 2008.

Herrnstein, Richard J., and Charles Murray. *The Bell Curve: Intelligence and Class Structure in American Life.* New York: Free Press, 1994.

Herskovits, Melville J. *The Myth of the Negro Past.* New York: Harper and Row, 1941.

Higginbotham, A. Leon. "Justice Clarence Thomas in Retrospect." *Hastings Law Journal* 45 (1984): 1405–27.

Hine, Darlene Clark, William C. Hine, and Stanley Harrold. *The African-American Odyssey.* 2nd ed. Upper Saddle River, NJ: Prentice Hall, 2004.

Hine, Darlene Clark, et al., eds. *"We Specialize in the Wholly Impossible": A Reader in Black Women's History.* New York: Carlson Publishing, 1995.

Holt, Thomas C. "The Political Uses of Alienation: W. E. B. Du Bois on Politics, Race, and Culture, 1903–1940."*American Quarterly* 42 (1990): 100–15. Reprinted in *Intellectuals and Public Life: Between Radicalism and Reform,* edited by Leon Fink, Stephen T. Leonard, and Michael Reid, 236–56. Ithaca, NY: Cornell UP 1996.

———. *The Problem of Race in the Twenty-first Century.* Cambridge, MA: Harvard UP, 2001.

———. "W. E. B. Du Bois's Archeology of Race: Re-reading the 'Conservation of the Races,'" In *W. E. B. Du Bois: Race and the City: The Philadelphia Negro and Its Legacy,* edited by Michael B. Katz and Thomas J. Sugrue. Philadelphia: U of Pennsylvania P, 1998.

———. "Whither Now and Why." In *The State Of Afro-American History: Past, Present, and Future,* edited by Darlene Clark Hine, 1–10. Baton Rouge: Louisiana State UP, 1986.

Hooks, bell. *Ain't I a Woman: Black Women and Feminism.* Boston: South End Press, 1981.

———. *Killing Rage: Ending Racism.* New York: Henry Holt, 1995.

Horne, Gerald. *Race War! White Supremacy and the Japanese Attack on the British Empire.* New York: New York UP, 2003.

Hotchkin, Sheila. "Henry Louis Gates Stays at Harvard." AP Online. 1 June 2002.

Huggins, Nathan I. *Harlem Renaissance.* New York: Oxford UP, 1971.

Hurston, Zora Neale. *Dust Tracks on a Road.* Chicago: U of Illinois P, 1985.

———. "How It Feels to Be Colored Me." *World Tomorrow*, 11 May 1928, 215–16.

Jackson, Lawrence. *Ralph Ellison: Emergence of Genius*. New York: Wiley, 2002.

Jackson, Walter A. *Gunnar Myrdal and America's Conscience: Social Engineering and Racial Liberalism, 1938–1987*. Chapel Hill: U North Carolina P, 1990.

James, Joy. *Transcending the Talented Tenth: Black Leaders and American Intellectuals*. New York: Routledge, 1996.

James, Winston. *Holding Aloft the Banner of Ethiopia: Caribbean Radicalism in the Early Twentieth Century America*. New York: Verso, 1998.

Janken, Kenneth Robert. *Rayford W. Logan and the Dilemma of the African American Intellectual*. Amherst: U of Massachusetts P, 1993.

Johnson, Charles. "The End of the Black American Narrative." *American Scholar* 9 (summer 2008): 32–42.

———. *Oxherding Tale*. New York: Blond and Briggs, 1983.

———. *Turning the Wheel: Essays on Buddhism and Writing*. New York: Scribner, 2003.

Johnson, James W. *Along This Way*. New York: Penguin Putnam, Viking, 1933. Reprint, *James Weldon Johnson: Writings*. New York: Library of America, 2004.

———. *Black Manhattan*. New York: Knopf, 1930.

Jones, Jacqueline. *Soldiers of Light and Love: Northern Teachers and Georgia Blacks, 1865–1873*. Athens: U of Georgia P, 1980.

Jordan, June. *Affirmative Acts*. New York: Doubleday, 1998.

———. *Some of Us Did Not Die: New and Selected Essays*. New York: Basic Civitas Books, 2003.

Joseph, Peniel E. *Waiting 'til the Midnight Hour: A Narrative History of the Black Power Movement*. New York: Henry Holt, 2006.

Kaplan, Carla, ed. *Zora Neale Hurston: A Life in Letters*. New York: Doubleday, 2002.

Katz, Michael, ed. *The "Underclass" Debate: Views from History*. Princeton, NJ: Princeton UP, 1993.

Kearney, Reginald. *African American Views of the Japanese: Solidarity or Sedition*. Albany: State U of New York P, 1998.

Keita, Meghan. *Race and the Writing of History: Riddling the Sphinx*. New York: Oxford UP, 2000.

Kelley, Robin D. G. *Freedom Dreams: The Black Radical Imagination*. Boston: Beacon, 2003.

———. *Race Rebels: Culture, Politics, and the Black Working Class*. New York: Free Press, 1994.

Kennedy, David M. *Freedom from Fear: The American People in Depression and War, 1929–1945*. New York: Oxford UP, 1999.

Kennedy, Randall. *Race, Crime, and the Law*. New York: Pantheon, 1997.

Kershaw, Ian. *Hitler, 1889–1936: Hubris*. New York: W. W. Norton, 1998.

———. *Hitler, 1936–1945: Nemesis*. New York: W. W. Norton, 2000.

Kete, Molefi Asante. *Afrocentric Idea*. Philadelphia: Temple UP, 1987.

Kilson, Martin. "Colin Powell: A Flight from Power?" *Dissent* 43, no. 2 (1996): 71–75.

———. "The Interaction of the Black Mainstream Leadership and the Farrakhan Extremists." In *Multi-America: Essays on Cultural Wars and Cultural Peace*, edited by Ishmael Reed, 238–45. New York: Viking, 1997.

———. "Styles of Black Intellectuals." *Black Renaissance/Renaissance Noir* 1, no. 3 (spring 1998): 50–82.

Kirby, John B. *Black Americans in the Roosevelt Era: Race and Liberalism.* Knoxville: U of Tennessee P, 1982.

Ladner, Joyce A. *The Death of White Sociology.* New York: Vintage, 1973.

Lemert, Charles, ed. *The Voice of Anna Julia Cooper: Including a Voice from the South and Other Important Essays, Papers, and Letters (Legacies of Social Thought).* New York: Rowman and Littlefield, 1998.

Lester, Julius. *All Is Well.* New York: William Morrow, 1976.

———. *And All Our Wounds Forgiven.* New York: Arcade, 1994.

———. "Black Racism," *A Commonplace Book,* http://acommonplacejbl.blogspot.com/2007/02/black-racism.html (5 Feb. 2007).

———. *Do Lord Remember Me.* New York: Henry Holt, 1984.

———. *Falling Pieces of the Broken Sky.* New York: Arcade, 1990.

———. "The Inauguration," *A Commonplace Book,* http://acommonplacejbl.blogspot.com (21 Jan. 2009.)

———. "Introduction." In *Black and White Reflections of a White Southern Sociologist,* by Lewis M. Killian. Lanham, MD: Rowman and Littlefield, 1994.

———. "The Mark of Race." *Civil Liberties Review,* January/February 1979, 115–18.

———. "The Time Has Come." *New Republic,* 28 Oct. 1985, 11–12.

———. *To Be a Slave.* New York: Scholastic, 1968.

———. "Why Black Americans Are Indebted to White Americans," *A Commonplace Book,* http://acommonplacejbl.blogspot/2008/why-black-americans-are-indebted-to.html (28 November 2008).

Leverence, John. *Irving Wallace: A Writer's Profile.* New York: Popular Press, 1974.

Levine, Lawrence W. *Black Culture and Black Consciousness: Afro-American Folk Thought from Slavery to Freedom.* New York: Oxford UP, 1977.

Lewis, David Levering. *W. E. B. Du Bois: Biography of a Race, 1868–1919.* New York: Holt Paperbacks, 1993.

———. *W. E. B. Du Bois: The Fight for Equality and the American Century, 1919–1963.* New York: Holt, 2000.

———. *When Harlem Was in Vogue.* New York: Vintage Books, 1982.

Lewis, David Levering, ed. *W. E. B. Du Bois: A Reader.* New York: Henry Holt, 1995.

Litwack, Leon. *Trouble in Mind: Black Southerners in the Age of Jim Crow.* New York: Knopf, 1998.

Loury, Glenn C. *One by One from the Inside Out: Essays and Reviews on Race and Responsibility in America.* New York: Free Press, 1995.

Malcolm X with Alex Haley. *The Autobiography of Malcolm X.* New York: Grove, 1964.

Marable, Manning. *Race, Reform, and Rebellion: The Second Reconstruction and Beyond in Black America, 1945–2006.* 3rd ed. Jackson: U of Mississippi P, 2007.

Marable, Manning, et al. *The Souls of W. E. B. Du Bois.* Boulder, CO: Paradigm, 2006.

March on Washington Committee. "Call to America: To March on Washington for Jobs and Equal Participation in National Defense." In *Reporting Civil Rights: Part One,* 1–4.

Margolick, David. *Beyond Glory: Joe Louis vs. Max Schmeling*. New York: Knopf, 2005.

Mauro, Tony. "Thomas Makes His Mark." *USA Today*, 6 July 2000, 15A.

Maxwell, William J. *New Negro, Old Left: African American Writing and Communism between the Wars*. New York: Columbia UP, 1999.

McAuley, Christopher A. *The Mind of Oliver C. Cox*. Notre Dame, IN: Notre Dame UP, 2004.

McGrath, Ben. "The Radical: Why Do Editors Keep Throwing 'The Boondocks' off the Funnies Page?" *New Yorker*, 19 April 2004. http://www.newyorker.com/archive/2004/04/19/040419fa_fact2.

McGruder, Aaron. *All the Rage: The Boondocks Past and Present*. New York: Three Rivers Press, 2007.

———. *The Boondocks: Cos I Know You Don't Read the Newspapers*. Riverside, NJ: Andrews McMeel Publishing, 2001.

———. *The Boondocks: The Complete First Season*. Directed by Anthony Bell. 323 min. Sony Pictures Home Entertainment, 2005. DVD.

———. *A Right to Be Hostile: The Boondocks Treasury*. New York: Three Rivers Press, 2003.

McNeil, Gena Rae. *Groundwork: Charles Houston and the Struggle for Civil Rights*. Philadelphia: U of Pennsylvania P, 1983.McPherson, James Alan. "Indivisible Man." In Callahan, *The Collected Essays of Ralph Ellison*, 355–95.

McWhorter, John. *Authentically Black: Essays for the New Black Silent Majority*. New York: Gotham Books, 2003.

———. *Losing the Race: Self Sabotage in Black America*. New York: Harper Perennial, 2001.

———. "Still Losing the Race." *Commentary* 117, no. 2 (2004): 37–41.

———. *Winning The Race: Beyond the Crisis in Black America*. New York: Gotham Books, 2005.

Meier, August, and Elliot Rudwick. *Black History and the Historical Profession, 1915–1980*. Urbana: U of Illinois P, 1986.

Miele, Frank. *Intelligence, Race, and Genetics: Conversations with Arthur R. Jensen*. Boulder, CO: Westview, 2002.

Morel, Lucas E. *Ralph Ellison and the Raft of Hope: A Political Companion to Invisible Man*. Lexington: UP of Kentucky, 2004.

Morrison, Toni. *Beloved*. New York: Alfred Knopf, 1987.

———. *Playing in the Dark: Whiteness and the Literary Imagination*. Cambridge: Harvard UP, 1992.

———. *Song of Solomon*. New York: Alfred Knopf, 1977.

Moses, Wilson Jeremiah. *Afrotopia: The Roots of African American Popular History*. Cambridge: Cambridge UP, 1998.

———. "Culture, Civilization, and the Decline of the West: The Afrocentrism of W. E. B. Du Bois." In *W. E. B. Dubois on Race and Culture*, edited by Bernard Bell, Emily R. Grosholz, and James B. Stewart. New York: Routledge, 1996.

———. *The Golden Age of Black Nationalism, 1850–1925*. New York: Oxford UP, 1988.

Moses, Wilson Jeremiah, ed. *Classical Black Nationalism: From the American Revolution to Marcus Garvey*. New York: New York UP, 1996.

Murray, Albert. *The Omni-Americans*. New York: Outerbridge and Dienstfrey, 1970.

Murray, Charles. *Losing Ground: American Social Policy, 1950–1980*. New York: Basic Books, 1984.

Murray, Pauli. "A Blueprint for First Class Citizenship: The Spirit of Revolt Took Shape, 1942–1944." In Carson et al., *Reporting Civil Rights*, 62–67.

Myrdal, Gunnar. *An American Dilemma: The Negro Problem and Modern Democracy*. 2 vols. New York: Harper, 1944.

New York Times. *Obama: The Historic Journey*. New York: Times Books, 2009.

Obama, Barack. *Dreams from My Father: A Story of Race and Inheritance*. New York: Three Rivers Press, 1995, 2004.

———. "A More Perfect Union," in New York Times, *Obama: The Historic Journey*, 104–9.

O'Reilly, Kenneth. *Nixon's Piano: Presidents and Racial Politics from Washington to Clinton*. New York: Free Press, 1995.

Ottley, Roi. "Seething with Resentment." In Carson et al., *Reporting Civil Rights: Part One*, 5–10.

Owens, Leslie. "The African in the Garden: New World Slavery and Its Lifelines." In Darlene Clark Hine, ed., *The State of Afro-American History: Past, Present, and Future*. 25–36. Baton Rouge: Louisiana State UP, 1986.

———. *This Species of Property: Slave Life and Culture in the Old South*. New York: Oxford UP, 1976.

Painter, Nell. "A Different Sense of Time." Rev. of *The Future of the Race*, by Henry Louis Gates Jr. and Cornel West. *Nation* 262, no. 18 (1996): 38–43.

Patterson, Orlando. "Blacklash." *Transition* 62 (1994): 4–27.

———. "The Eternal Revolution." *New York Times*, op. ed., 7 Nov. 2008, A35.

———. *The Ordeal of Integration: Progress and Resentment in America's "Racial" Crisis*. New York: Basic Civitas, 1998.

Pierce, Ponchitta. "What Is Not So Funny about the Funnies." *Ebony* 22 (November 1966): 48–56.

Platt, Anthony M. *E. Franklin Frazier Reconsidered*. New Brunswick, NJ: Rutgers UP, 1991.

Posner, Richard. *Public Intellectuals: A Study of Decline*. Cambridge, MA: Harvard UP, 2002.

Posnock, Ross. *Color and Culture: Black Writers and the Making of Modern Intellectuals*. Cambridge, MA: Harvard UP, 1998.

Quarles, Benjamin. *The Negro in the Making of America*. 1964. 3rd ed. New York: Touchstone, 1987.

Rampersad, Arnold. *The Life of Langston Hughes, 1902–1941*, vol. 1: *I, Too, Sing America*. New York: Oxford UP, 1986.

———. *The Life of Langston Hughes, 1941–1967*, vol. 2: *I Dream A World*. New York: Oxford UP, 1988.

———. *Ralph Ellison: A Biography*. New York: Knopf, 2007.

"Readers Forum: Replies to Eugene Rivers 'Nationalism of Fools.'" *Boston Review* 20, no. 4 (1995): 24–30.

Reed, Adolph, Jr. *The Jesse Jackson Phenomenon: The Crisis of Purpose on Afro-American Politics*. New Haven, CT: Yale UP, 1986.

———. "The Rise of Louis Farrakhan." In *Class Notes: Posing as Politics and Other Thoughts on the American Scene*. 37–60. New York: New Press, 2000.

Remnick, David. "Dr. Wilson's Neighborhood." *New Yorker*, 29 April and 6 May 1996, 96–104.

Rivers, Eugene F., III. "Beyond the Nationalism of Fools: Toward an Agenda for Black Intellectuals." *Boston Review* 20, no. 3 (1995): 16–18.

———. "On the Responsibility of Intellectuals in the Age of Crack." *Boston Review* 17, no. 14 (September–October 1992): 3–4.

Robinson, Cedric. *Black Marxism*. Chapel Hill: U of North Carolina P, 2000.

Robinson, Greg. "Ralph Ellison, Albert Murray, Stanley Crouch, and Modern Black Conservatism." In *Black Conservatism: Essays in Intellectual and Political History*, edited by Peter Eisenstadt, 151–67. New York: Routledge, 1998.

Rorty, Richard. *Philosophy and Social Hope*. London: Penguin Books, 1999.

Rowley, Hazel. *Richard Wright: The Life and Times*. New York: Henry Holt, 2001.

Sacks, Macy S. *Before Harlem: The Black Experience in New York City before World War I*. Philadelphia: U of Pennsylvania P, 2006.

Said, Edward W. *Representations of the Intellectual*. New York: Pantheon Books, 1994.

Savage, William W., Jr. *Commies, Cowboys, and Jungle Queens: Comic Books and America, 1945–1954*. Middleton, CT: Wesleyan UP, 1990.

Sawhill, Ray. "Black and Right." (Interview with Thomas Sowell.) Salon.com. 10 Nov. 1999.

Schuyler, George S. *Black and Conservative: The Autobiography of George S. Schuyler*. New Rochelle, NY: Arlington House, 1966.

———. "The Negro Art Hokum." Reprinted in *The Portable Harlem Renaissance Reader*, edited by David Levering Lewis, 96–99. New York: Viking Penguin, 1994.

Scott, Daryl M. *Contempt and Pity: Social Policy and the Image of the Damaged Black Psyche, 1880–1996*. Chapel Hill: U of North Carolina P, 1997.

Singh, Nikhil Pal. *Black Is a Country: Race and the Unfinished Struggle for Democracy*. Cambridge, MA: Harvard UP 2004.

———. "Negro Exceptionalism: The Antinomies of Harold Cruse." In *Harold Cruse's The Crisis of the Negro Intellectual Revisited*, edited by Jerry Gafio Watts, 73–93. New York: Routledge, 2004.

Sitkoff, Harvard. *A New Deal for Blacks: The Emergence of Civil Rights as a National Issue: The Depression Decade*. New York: Oxford UP, 1978.

———. *The Struggle for Black Equality, 1954–1992*. New York: Hill and Wang, 1993.

Sleeper, Jim. *Liberal Racism*. New York: Viking Adult, 1997.

Smethurst, James. "The Adventures of a Social Poet: Langston Hughes from the Popular Front to Black Power." In Tracy, *A Historical Guide to Langston Hughes*, 141–68.

Smethurst, James Edward. *The Black Arts Movement: Literary Nationalism in the 1960s and 1970s*. Chapel Hill: U of North Carolina P, 2005.

Sowell, Thomas. *Barbarians Inside the Gates*. Stanford, CA: Hoover Institution, 1999.

———. *The Economics and Politics of Race: An International Perspective*. New York: Harper Perennial, 1985.

———. *A Man of Letters*. New York: Encounter Books, 2007.

———. *A Personal Odyssey*. New York: Free Press, 2002.

Steele, Shelby. *A Bound Man: Why We Are Excited about Obama and Why He Can't Win.* New York: Free Press, 2007.

———. *The Content of Our Character: A New Vision of Race in America.* New York: Harper Perennial, 1991.

———. *A Dream Deferred: The Second Betrayal of Black Freedom in America.* New York: Harper Collins, 1998.

———. *White Guilt: How Blacks and Whites Together Destroyed the Promise of the Civil Rights Era.* New York: Harper Perennial, 2007.

Strömberg, Frederik. *Black Images in the Comics: A Visual History.* Seattle: Fantagraphics Books, 2003.

Stuckey, Sterling. *Slave Culture: Nationalist Theory and the Foundations of Black America.* New York: Oxford UP, 1987.

Sullivan, Patricia. *Days of Hope: Race and Democracy in the New Deal Era.* Chapel Hill: U of North Carolina P, 1996.

Talalay, Kathryn. *Composition in Black and White: The Life of Phillipa Schuyler.* New York: Oxford UP, 1995.

Tanenhaus, Sam. "The Ivy League's Angry Star." *Vanity Fair* 502 (June 2002): 200–203, 218–23.

Tracy, Steven C., ed. *A Historical Guide to Langston Hughes.* New York: Oxford UP, 2004.

Trotter, Joe William, Jr., "From a Raw Deal to a New Deal: 1929–1945." In Robin D. G. Kelley and Earl Lewis, eds., *To Make Our World Anew: A History of African Americans from 1890.* Vol. 2. New York: Oxford UP, 2005.

Walker, Alice. *The Color Purple.* New York: Harcourt Brace Jovanovich, 1982.

———. *In Search of Our Mothers' Gardens: Womanist Prose.* New York: Harcourt, 1983.

———. "Looking for Zora," in *In Search of Our Mothers' Gardens.*

———. "White House Advice." *Newsweek Inauguration Issue,* 27 Jan. 2009, 106–8.

Walker, Margaret. *Richard Wright: Daemonic Genius.* New York: Warner Books, 1988.

Wallace, Michele. *Invisibility Blues.* New York: Verso, 1991.

Ward, Brian. *Just My Soul Responding: Rhythm and Blues, Black Consciousness, and Race Relations.* Berkeley: U of California P, 1998.

Warren, Kenneth W. "Ralph Ellison and the Problem of Cultural Authority: The Lessons of Little Rock." Chap. 7 in Morel, *Ralph Ellison and the Raft of Hope.*

———. *So Black and Blue: Ralph Ellison and the Occasion of Criticism.* Chicago: U of Chicago P, 2003.

Watts, Jerry Gafio. *Heroism and the Black Intellectual: Ralph Ellison, Politics, and Afro-American Intellectual Life.* Chapel Hill: U of North Carolina P, 1994.

———. "The Souls of Black Folks and Afro-American Intellectual Life." In Marable et al., *The Souls of W. E. B. Du Bois,* 98–135.

Weisbrot, Robert. *Freedom Bound: A History of America's Civil Rights Movement.* New York: W. W. Norton, 1990.

West, Cornel. *The Cornel West Reader.* New York: Basic Civitas Books, 1999.

———. "The Dilemma of the Black Intellectual." Chap. 19 in *The Cornel West Reader.*

———. *Hope on a Tightrope: Words and Wisdom.* Carlsbad, CA: Hay House, 2008.

———. "Integration at the Top," *Newsweek Inauguration Issue*, 27 Jan. 2009, 116–18.

———. "On the 1980s." Chap. 22 in *The Cornel West Reader*.

———. "Parents and National Survival." Chap. 21 in *The Cornel West Reader*.

———. *Prophetic Fragments: Illuminations of the Crisis in American Religion and Culture*. Grand Rapids, MI: Wm. B. Eerdmans, 1988.

———. *Race Matters*. Boston, MA: Beacon, 1993.

West, Cornel, and bell hooks. *Breaking Bread: Insurgent Black Intellectual Life*. Boston, MA: South End Press, 1991.

West, Michael Rudolph. *The Education of Booker T. Washington: American Democracy and the Idea of Race Relations*. New York: Columbia UP, 2006.

White, Deborah Grey. *Ar'n't I a Woman: Female Slaves in the Plantation South*. New York: W. W. Norton, 1985.

Wieseltier, Leon. "All and Nothing at All." *New Republic*, 6 Mar. 1995, 31.

Williams, Juan. *Thurgood Marshall, American Revolutionary*. New York: Crown, 1998.

Williams, Lena. "Black Women's Book Starts a Predictable Storm." *New York Times*, 2 Oct. 1990, C14–15.

Williams, Oscar R. *George S. Schuyler: Portrait of a Black Conservative*. Knoxville: U of Tennessee P, 2007.

Williams, Patricia. *The Alchemy of Race and Rights: Diary of a Law Professor*. Cambridge: Harvard UP, 1991.

———. *The Rooster's Egg: On the Persistence of Prejudice*. Cambridge: Harvard UP, 1995.

Williams, Vernon J., Jr., *Re-Thinking Race: Franz Boas and His Contemporaries*. Lexington: UP of Kentucky, 1996.

Wilson, Francille R. *The Segregated Scholars: Black Social Scientists and the Creation of Black Labor Studies, 1890–1950*. Charlottesville: U of Virginia P, 2006.

Wilson, Robib. "The Power of Professors." *Chronicle of Higher Education*, 3 Mar. 2006, A10–13.

Wilson, William Julius. *The Declining Significance of Race: Blacks and Changing American Institutions*. Chicago: U of Chicago P, 1978.

———. *More than Just Race: Being Black and Poor in the Inner-City*. New York: W. W. Norton, 2009.

———. *The Truly Disadvantaged*. Chicago: U of Chicago P, 1987.

———. *When Work Disappears: The World of the New Urban Poor*. New York: Knopf, 1996.

Wright, Kai, ed., *The African American Experience: Black History and Culture Through Speeches, Letters, Editorials, Poems, Songs, and Stories*. New York: Black Dog and Leventhal Publishers, 2001, 2009.

Wright, Richard. *Black Boy: (American Hunger) a Record of Childhood and Youth*. New York: HarperCollins, 2005.

———. *Uncle Tom's Children: Four Novellas*. New York: Harper, 1938.

Young, James O. *Black Writers of the Thirties*. Baton Rouge: Louisiana State UP, 1973.

INDEX

abolitionists, black, 120
abortion issue, 78–79
Abraham Lincoln Brigades, 19
Abrams, Morris, 77
Abyssinian Baptist Church, 80
accommodationism, 39, 56
affirmative action, 7, 52, 107; black
    conservative attacks on, 79–80; Rea-
    gan era attacks on, 76–80; as reverse
    discrimination, 69, 100
Africana encyclopedia, 8
African American intellectuals: *Ameri-
    can Dilemma* and, 37–48; black
    critiques of, 42–43; capabilities
    questioned, 108, 110–13; complex-
    ity of, 1–2; cultural relativism and,
    23–24; distance from black masses,
    26, 41, 60, 114; divergent ideologies,
    55, 124; historically grounded, 1–2;
    insurgent black intellectual, 108–9;
    late twentieth century, 45, 114; liter-
    ary thinkers, 20; marginalization
    of, 45, 53; moral capital and, 44–46,
    50–51, 54–55, 58, 114, 132n. 49;
    questioning of, 108–12; role in major
    revolutions, 44–45; role in revealing
    American truth, 6; 1980s, 52–53;
    shifts in thinking, 30, 49–50, 63–64,
    68–69; as transformative black in-
    telligentsia, 124, 141n. 49; women,
    8, 47–48, 52, 61, 100, 106. *See also*
    conservative intellectuals, African
    American; public intellectuals
African Americans: black presence, 6,
    14; definitions of, 119–21; outside
    South, 17–18. *See also* family, Afri-
    can American
African Blood Brotherhood, 21
Africanism, 88
Afro-Asiatic connection, 33

Afro-British scholars, 106
Afro-Caribbeans, 17, 21, 27, 91
Afrocentricity, 95–96
Afrocentrism, 3–4, 88
Ali, Scheherazade, 74–75
Along This Way (Johnson), 19–20
Als, Hilton, 109
American creed, appeals to, 36, 38
*American Dilemma, An: The Negro
    Problem and Modern Democracy*
    (Myrdal), 28, 37–40, 48
American Historical Association, 109
American identity, 18; Africanism,
    88; binary notion of race, 98;
    Civil Rights movement, impact
    on, 89–90; composite nation, 86;
    multiracial, 108, 114, 119; Obama's
    Democratic National Convention
    speech, 116–17
American Missionary Association, 46
American Negro Academy, 14
Ames, Lloyd, 36
Amsterdam News, 33, 101
And All Our Wounds Forgiven (Lester),
    89–90
Anderson, Elijah, 55
Angelou, Maya, 100
Ani, Marimba, 58
anticommunism, 29–30, 31, 68, 91–92
Antioch Review, 40
anti-Semitism, 58, 61, 73–74, 75
Appiah, Kwame Anthony, 109, 112
art, 13, 86; black arts movement,
    93–94, 99
Asante, Molefi, 58
assimilation, 25–26, 29
Atlantic Monthly, 14
Atlantic Records, 92
Axis powers, 33
Azusa Pentecostal Church, 80

CHARLES PETE BANNER-HALEY, an associate professor of history and Africana and Latin American studies at Colgate University, is the author of *To Do Good and to Do Well: Middle Class Blacks and the Depression, Philadelphia, 1929–1941*, and *The Fruits of Integration: Black Middle-Class Ideology and Culture, 1960–1990*, as well as more than a dozen articles. He is the former director of Colgate's Africana–Latin American studies program.